MYSTERIES OF THE NIGHT

A FRESH PERSPECTIVE ON DREAMS

Daniel answered the king and said, "No wise men, enchanters, magicians, or astrologers can show to the king the mystery that the king has asked, but there is a God in heaven who reveals mysteries... But as for me, this mystery has been revealed to me, not because of any wisdom that I have more than all the living, but in order that the interpretation may be made known to the king, and that you may know the thoughts of your mind... The king answered and said to Daniel, "Truly, your God is God of gods and Lord of kings, and a revealer of mysteries for you have been able to reveal this mystery."
Daniel 2:27-28a, 30, 47

MYSTERIES OF THE NIGHT

A FRESH PERSPECTIVE ON DREAMS

BY

Barbara Kain Parker

Mysteries of the Night

MYSTERIES OF THE NIGHT
A FRESH PERSPECTIVE ON DREAMS

Barbara Kain Parker

Aslan's Place Publications
9315 Sagebrush Street
Apple Valley, CA 92308
760-810-0990
aslansplace.com

All Rights Reserved. No part of this book may be reproduced or transmitted in any form or by any means—electronic or mechanical, including photocopying, recording, or by any information storage and retrieval system—without written permission from the authors except as provided by the copyright laws of the United States of America. Unauthorized reproduction is a violation of both federal and spiritual laws.

Unless otherwise indicated, scriptures are taken from the: The ESV® Bible (The Holy Bible, English Standard Version®) copyright © 2001 by Crossway Bible, a publishing ministry of Good News Publishers. Used by permission. All rights reserved.

Copyright 2022, by Barbara Kain Parker
All rights reserved.
Editor: Barbara Kain Parker
Cover Design: Brodie Schmidtke

ISBN: 979-8-3699-0038-3

Printed in the United states of America

DEDICATION

With love and gratitude, *Mysteries of the Night: A Fresh Perspective on Dreams* is dedicated to Briana Lassiter and her daughter, Jackie; without whom much of this book would never have been written.

Oil and perfume make the heart glad, and the sweetness of a friend comes from his earnest counsel.
Proverbs 27:9

ENDORSEMENTS

If you think you have read everything there is to read about dreams, you have not. *Mysteries of the Night* is not just another book about dreams. In this masterful work, Barbara Parker has explored the depth and complexities of dream from a solid Biblical foundation. After you have read this book, you will be motivated to reexamine your dreams in light of ground breaking revelation, and then you will be blessed with a new understanding of how much the Lord loves talking to you through your dreams.

Paul L Cox
Aslan's Place; Apple Valley, CA
Co-founder of The Kingdom Institute; Aiea, HI
https://aslansplace.com

I believe that in the coming generations, we will see an increase in the pouring out of the Spirit of Jesus. It is not enough for spiritual babies to raise spiritual babies - it's time for the Beef; and friends, Barbara's books are some of the choicest cuts. For myself, my wife and our daughters, she has lifted the veil to a more intimate walk with Jesus. We have been delighted to discover that we are all dreamers; and as a result of her life-long pursuit of the Father, we have entered a new frontier of dreams together; and for the first time, we are unafraid. *Mysteries of the Night* will unlock your next flight for inter-dimensional travel, a stronger and deeper Biblical understanding of the dream world, and wisdom in the secret heart. Be encouraged: the One speaks!

A Fresh Perspective on Dreams

He has the most precious and intimate things to say to you tonight.

Byron Williams
Worship Director; Aslan's Place Intern
Houston, Texas

All of us experience dreams in the night – some regularly, some rarely. We know this is one of the ways God communicates with us. But how skilled are we at interpreting and understanding the mysteries of the night?

Barbara Parker's new book is an insightful, helpful, and accessible guide for anyone looking to develop in dream interpretation. Peppered with solid biblical references and real-life stories, you will be encouraged, strengthened, and empowered to recognize, hear, and understand the voice of God. For parents and grandparents or those working with young people, we particularly recommend the chapters on 'children and dream interpretation' to help navigate conversation and bring understanding to our children or grandchildren's dream world.

As ones involved in pastoral ministry and church leadership for over thirty years, we would have benefitted from this book much sooner! We are delighted to recommend *Mysteries of the Night* as a must for every bookshelf or library.

Nigel & Louise Reid
Wicklow, Ireland

Mysteries of the Night

This book is a wonderful aid for the times we live in. It is a door opener not only for those who are familiar with dreams and their interpretations, but also those of us who do not consider ourselves dreamers. We read so often in the Bible about the many times God speaks to his people, prophets, and even gentile Kings through dreams; yet so many of us treat our dreams like 'junk mail'.

The author takes us on a journey of deep revelation, and at the same time challenges our preconceptions and encourages us to think afresh about the whole topic. As we approach the time of steel, as in the four creatures of Daniel 7, and we see our culture hardening in attitudes, being altered, warring against itself, remaking nature and gender; we must not underestimate the significance of the dreams God gives us. His dreams and their meaning are our daily bread, giving us entry to the deep mysteries of His kingdom as He opens His heart; showing us the way He sees things.

When we consider how much of our lives are spent sleeping, how much more should we be asking the Lord to invade our dreams? This book will teach you a healthy honour for your dreams, excite you with the power of dreams, and open up the realms of walking in the supernatural power of God in the realm of dreams.

Paul Knight
Composer; Actor; Musician
London, England
https://www.paulwknightmusic.com/home

A Fresh Perspective on Dreams

Prophetic Word

Welcome to my new day. Welcome to a fresh new way.

There is a rumbling out of the depths of the ancient oil of My Spirit that was upon people of old, like Joseph, to interpret dreams.

This is a shift of impartation to come upon My Holy Nation to interpret strategy from the hidden parables of dreams and visions. It's time to arise and be clothed afresh with strength. Come see with me, out of the mystery of all that I AM, that which is about to be revealed in the Earth. I'm kissing my dreamers awake to a level of authority that has not been seen in this century.

Draw near to me and I will anoint your dreams to see what I desire; to be and to release in the consecrated Body of My resurrected Son. Arise, and let your eyes be anointed with ancient oil. Come!

Larry Pearson
Lion Sword Solutions
Niagara-on-the-Lake, Ontario, Canada
https://www.lionswordsolutions.ca/

Mysteries of the Night

A Fresh Perspective on Dreams

TABLE OF CONTENTS

Foreword	*13*
Introduction	*15*
Chapter One: The Gift of Dreaming	*19*
Chapter Two: Dream Devaluation	*27*
Chapter Three: Old Dreams Made New	*37*
Chapter Four: Clues & Life	*53*
Chapter Five Dream Killers in Disguise	*59*
chapter Six: True or False?	*73*
Chapter Seven: Dream Hackers	*81*
Chapter Eight: Teach Your Children Well	*99*
Chapter Nine: A Heart for Every Generation	*109*
Chapter Ten: Through the Eyes of a Child	*117*
Chapter Eleven: Fantastical Faith	*125*
Chapter Twelve: God's Social Networking	*141*
Chapter Thirteen: Love Letters From God	*151*
Chapter Fourteen: And Yet, there's More	*155*
Conclusion	*163*

Mysteries of the Night

A Fresh Perspective on Dreams

FOREWORD

In 1997, I attended a weekday seminar led by Mike Bickel; and he wrapped up his message that day by imparting the prophetic spirit to some of us in the room. To my delight, the next morning I had my first prophetic dream, although I wasn't sure of its meaning. In the days, weeks and months that followed, I had so many dreams that I realized that the Father wanted me to record them in a three-ring binder. So, I diligently wrote down my dreams; but I must confess that even though I was excited that the Father was speaking to me, I was also frustrated because I couldn't decipher what the dreams meant. I had prophetic sight (the dreams), but not prophetic insight (the interpretation of the mysteries of the night).

A few years later, my friend and colleague, Dr. Paul Cox, introduced me to Barbara Parker at a conference at Aslan's Place in Apple Valley, California. Over the years, I have grown to greatly appreciate Barbara, who is not only a gifted author and anointed dream interpreter, but also a friend and great encouragement to me personally. With that said Barbara's latest book, ***Mysteries of the Night,*** is a must-read if you have concluded that your dreams are the result of eating bad pizza. It will also be a helpful resource if you desire to get to the next level of understanding the mysteries of the kingdom.

Although time and space do not permit me to share in detail the hidden treasures I found in this book, I can say without reservation that if you apply the insights in this prophetic work, they will guide you into the abundant life. In Chapter 2 for example, Barbara clearly explains how the enemy works overtime to convince us that our dreams have no value, while Chapter 3 strategically delves into how stinking thinking, personal sin and emotions like fear and worry block us from hearing our Heavenly Father speaking to us on a regular basis. I also found Barbara's chapter about how to help our children understand their dreams to be vitally important for training the next generation to hear and understand the voice of God.

The bottom line is this: If you hope to grow in your working knowledge of dream interpretation and, more importantly, desire to grow in intimacy with the Father, order a copy of this book. It is a life-changing guide and a wonderful source of wisdom.

Rob Gross
Senior Pastor, Mountain View Community Church
Co-founder of The Kingdom Institute
Aiea, Hawaii

A Fresh Perspective on Dreams

INTRODUCTION

The Lord first spoke to me about writing a book about dreams in 2017, and *Exploring Heavenly Places, Volume 8: Dreamspeak* was the result. From its introduction:

> "Write a book about dream interpretation for the *Exploring Heavenly Places* series." There was a spark of excitement at the thought, but I had to ask, "Who, me? Write about dreams? What would I write, Lord? What can be said that has not already been written? You know there are already lots of resources available about dream interpretation, many of which are on my bookshelf, and most are very much the same."
>
> I explained to the Lord that I was willing, but I would need to rely on Him for inspiration so the book wouldn't read like a re-tread.

Five years later, and it's happened again; now it's, "Write another book on dreams." Aside from ac couple chapters that will be based on a previously written stand-alone article, I am at a loss regarding how to proceed. Still with a shelf full of excellent dream resources, I remain completely dependent on the Holy Spirit to deliver a fresh perspective on dreams.

> *Now we have received not the spirit of the world, but the Spirit who is from God, that we might understand*

> *the things freely given us by God. And we impart this in words not taught by human wisdom but taught by the Spirit, interpreting spiritual truths to those who are spiritual.*[1]

I have a journaling Bible with margins that are full of notes going back over many years; a Bible that's been used so much that it was coming apart, and I had to re-glue the spine of the pages to the leather cover. Reading through that Bible, I am often shocked at how many things have been recorded over the years that I've completely forgotten about. Sometimes it's an insight that the Spirit gave me; other times it's a comment, such as a point I might make if I were teaching; other times it's a date referencing a journal entry or a dream that has vanished from my memory. I'm often left in awe, wondering how I knew that, or how I figured something out. Clearly though, it wasn't me; rather, my mind was enlightened by the Spirit of the Lord, who is my Teacher.

There can be no doubt that much of what we've experienced or learned throughout our lives has long been forgotten; especially as we age, and year after year of memories get stacked one on top of another. The truth of this was reinforced to me recently as I began going through old journals. That I was astounded is an understatement! There were people I'd mentioned by their initials and could no longer remember the specific conversations, let alone their names. There were also many wonderful memories that have long been stored in my memory banks somewhere, just waiting to be re-awakened. Then there were the dreams; oh, so many dreams!

The Lord had already given me the sub-title for this book, but I'd been second-guessing it; wondering if it was really Him and if I should try to come up with something better. With the book about half finished at the moment, I've also been wondering what I could write in this Introduction; until just a few minutes ago, that is, when I finally got my 'ah-ha'. The Teacher showed me that just as I often go back and re-visit the margins of my Bible to get a fresh perspective on an old truth, the book is meant to provide *A Fresh Perspective on Dreams*.

The perspective offered here is a mixed bag of what you may already know that is approached from, perhaps, a different angle. Included are new insights we've received over the past few years at Aslan's Place regarding dreams, the inclusion of some exciting content that was gained through the eyes of a child, and a look back at old dreams to gain new understanding.

My prayer is that you will be inspired to travel into new realms of understanding regarding dreams from a fresh, God-given perspective, and that the Lord will use this book to spark new levels of excitement regarding His gift of dreaming.

Barbara Kain Parker

Mysteries in the Night

---

[1] 1 Corinthians 2:12-13

Chapter One:
The Gift of Dreaming

Dreams and the ability to understand them are a God-given gift; they are priceless treasures. Perhaps we have not even realized that He speaks through dreams just as surely as any other manner in which we hear His voice, but Scripture is clear:

> *For God speaks in one way, and in two, though man does not perceive it. In a dream, in a vision of the night…*[1]

King Saul understood the value of dreams. He'd started well as Israel's first king, but in choosing to rely on himself instead of obeying God, he lost the kingdom after he made a fatal mistake:

> *And Samuel said, "Has the LORD as great delight in burnt offerings and sacrifices, as in obeying the voice of the LORD? Behold, to obey is better than sacrifice, and to listen than the fat of rams. For rebellion is as the sin of divination, and presumption is as iniquity and idolatry. Because you have rejected the word of the LORD, he has also rejected you from being king."* [2]

Eventually, desperation drove Saul even further into disobedience. After Samuel's death, he was frantic for prophetic insight so he visited the witch of Endor and convinced her to call up the spirit of Samuel:

> *Then Samuel said to Saul, "Why have you disturbed me by bringing me up?" Saul answered, "I am in great distress, for the Philistines are warring against me, and God has turned away from me and answers me no more, either by prophets or by dreams. Therefore I have summoned you to tell me what I shall do."* [3]

Saul had forgotten from Whom his blessings came, and paid a heavy price; to the point he couldn't even hear clearly from the Lord any longer.

In contrast, consider Daniel who, though hauled off into captivity, chose to adhere to his faith in the God of Abraham, Isaac and Jacob; this in spite of the rampant idolatry of Babylon. Though God had given him understanding of all dreams and visions,[4] he never once failed to acknowledge his Source, even at the risk of his own life:

> *Because of this the king was angry and very furious, and commanded that all the wise men of Babylon be destroyed. So the decree went out, and the wise men were about to be killed; and they sought Daniel and his companions, to kill them... Then Daniel went to his house and made the matter known to Hananiah, Mishael, and Azariah, his companions, and told them to seek mercy from the God of heaven concerning this mystery, so that Daniel and his companions might not be destroyed with the rest of the wise men of Babylon. Then the mystery was revealed to Daniel in a vision of the night. Then Daniel blessed the God of heaven...The king*

> *declared to Daniel, whose name was Belteshazzar, "Are you able to make known to me the dream that I have seen and its interpretation?" Daniel answered the king and said, "No wise men, enchanters, magicians, or astrologers can show to the king the mystery that the king has asked, but there is a God in heaven who reveals mysteries, and he has made known to King Nebuchadnezzar what will be in the latter days.[5]*

God's words always come with a purpose, so it makes sense that we need to pay attention to our dreams if we are to reap the benefit of His messages that arrive during sleep:

> *As the rain and the snow come down from heaven, and do not return to it without watering the earth and making it bud and flourish, so that it yields seed for the sower and bread for the eater, so is my word that goes out from my mouth: It will not return to me empty, but will accomplish what I desire and achieve the purpose for which I sent it.[6]*

William Branham, the famous evangelist known for conducting healing revivals in the mid-1960s, understood the gift of dreaming. A questioner once asked whether or not his prophetic dreams were a gift from God. Branham answered:

> The Lord bless you. That is, to my opinion, the gift of God. It's a gift of God. Don't you know the Bible speaks of dreams?

Joseph, how he dreamed of dreams and interpreted, and how others dreamed dreams. Those things are of God. Now, if it's of God, it'll always be truthful, it'll always happen just exactly the way He said.

And now don't…If you start showing off with it, it'll just leave you. See, just be reverent and sweet. And when He shows you anything, and it's something that you should tell somebody, that they've done something that's wrong, then just don't stand right up and rebuke that person, go to them yourself and say, "Sister, brother, you know, the Lord told me the other night that–that you were doing something wrong, a certain thing."

If that person says, "You are wrong! That is a lie! I did not do that!" Now, the thing to do then [is to go] back and say, "Heavenly Father, was that wrong?"

Now, if that person was telling you the truth, then you've got the wrong spirit. But if that person was lying, and he did do it, God will deal with that person. See? Yes, sir. Because see, what he's done there, he's blasphemed against the Holy Ghost, denying what the Holy Ghost has called to his attention. See here? So it's the wrong thing.[7]

Scriptures are clear that we are to value the gifts that the Lord bestows upon us so, having established that includes dreams, we'd do well to apply the following passages to them:

> *As each has received a <u>gift</u>, use it to serve one another, as good stewards of God's varied grace: whoever speaks, as one who speaks oracles of God; whoever serves, as one who serves by the strength that God supplies – in order that in everything God may be glorified through Jesus Christ. To him belong glory and dominion forever and ever. Amen.[8]*

> *Now there are varieties of <u>gifts</u>, but the same Spirit; and there are varieties of service, but the same Lord; and there are varieties of activities, but it is the same God who empowers them all in everyone. To each is given the manifestation of the Spirit for the common good.[9]*

> *Do not be deceived, my beloved brothers. Every good <u>gift</u> and every perfect <u>gift</u> is from above, coming down from the Father of lights, with whom there is no variation or shadow due to change.[10]*

Sadly, cessationist theology, accepted by many Christians, teaches that the gifts of the Spirit (i.e., tongues, prophecy, healing, miracles) were only for the apostolic age, that they passed away with the early Church and are not for today. Dreams and visions often get lumped into that doctrinal view, which would mean that they are of no spiritual benefit. But the Bible is clear:

> *But this is what was uttered through the prophet Joel: "And in the last days it shall be, God declares, that I will pour out my Spirit on all flesh, and your sons and your daughters shall prophesy, and your young men shall see*

visions, and your old men shall dream dreams; even on my male servants and female servants in those days I will pour out my Spirit, and they shall prophesy." [11]

And it shall come to pass afterward, that I will pour out my Spirit on all flesh; your sons and your daughters shall prophesy, your old men shall dream dreams, and your young men shall see visions.[12]

Most of us have probably never heard of Phillip Paul Bliss, a friend of D. L. Moody and a well-known gospel composer/singer in the 1800s. Lovers of old hymns will probably remember such songs as *Hallelujah, What a Saviour, Wonderful Words of Life,* and *Almost Persuaded*. But there's another one, *Dare to be a Daniel,* which was written for children, a portion of which follows:

> Standing by a purpose true,
> Heeding God's command,
> Honor them, the faithful few!
> All hail to Daniel's band!
>
> *Refrain:*
> Dare to be a Daniel,
> Dare to stand alone!
> Dare to have a purpose firm!
> Dare to make it known.
>
> Many mighty men are lost
> Daring not to stand,
> Who for God had been a host
> By joining Daniel's band.

Refrain:
Dare to be a Daniel,
Dare to stand alone!
Dare to have a purpose firm!
Dare to make it known.

Who will we dare to be? Will we, like King Saul, lose sight of our unchanging God, who bestows all manner of blessings and gifts upon us? Or, will we choose to stand firm in our faith and 'dare to be a Daniel', a faithful servant who lived many years and prospered under multiple kings, the man who fearlessly testified to King Nebuchadnezzar, "There is a God in heaven who reveals mysteries."

---

[1] Job 33:14-15a

[2] 1 Samuel 15:22-23

[3] 1 Samuel 28:15

[4] Daniel 1:17

[5] Daniel 2:12-13, 17-19, 27-28a

[6] Isaiah 55:10-11

[7] https://endtimesmessages.com/spiritual-gift-of-dreams-and-visions/

[8] 1 Peter 4:10-11

[9] 1 Corinthians 12:4-7

[10] James 1:16-17

[11] Hebrews 13:8

[12] Acts 2:16-18

Mysteries in the Night

Chapter Two:
Dream Devaluation

In an economic sense:

> Devaluation is the deliberate downward adjustment of the value of a country's money relative to another currency, group of currencies, or currency standard. Countries that have a fixed exchange rate or semi-fixed exchange rate use this monetary policy tool. It is often confused with depreciation and is the opposite of revaluation, which refers to the readjustment of a currency's exchange rate.[1]

In a spiritual sense, the enemy seeks to twist God's truths, steal everything he can, and destroy all that he can get his hands on:

> *The thief comes only to steal and kill and destroy. I came that they may have life and have it abundantly.*[2]

Does it not make sense then, that the devil would pull out all the stops to convince us that our dreams have no value? Remember, as with the devaluation of money, this is a deliberate downward adjustment of our God-given gift of dreaming; as the father of lies, there is no truth in him, and he seems to be endlessly creative when it comes to strategizing ways to steal, kill and destroy. While we may be righteous warriors for the cause of Christ on many battle fronts, if we succumb to his tricks regarding dreams, we are apt to lose the skirmish over ownership of one of our most effective weapons. Though our dreams should be cherished, they are devalued when we speak or think negatively about them. Therefore, it would be wise to avoid such sentiments as:

- I never dream
- My crazy dreams can't be relevant
- My dreams are often frightening, so I'd rather not dream at all
- My dreams don't make any sense; I'll never understand them

Our words matter. What we say, or even think, is often what we get:

> *Evildoers are trapped by their sinful talk, and so the innocent escape trouble. From the fruit of their lips people are filled with good things, and the work of their hands brings them reward.* [3]

> *But I tell you that everyone will have to give account on the day of judgment for every empty word they have spoken. For by your words you will be acquitted, and by your words you will be condemned.*[4]

> *May these words of my mouth and this meditation of my heart be pleasing in your sight, LORD, my Rock and my Redeemer.*[5]

Another common method of dream devaluation is believing the enemy's lies, which many in the Church have bought into. I can't even count the number of times I've heard, "Oh, that's New Age! I won't have anything to do with dream interpretation." Hmmm, seems like somebody forgot that the devil does everything in his power to corrupt, imitate and steal what God has created for good:

> *Why do you not understand what I say? It is because you cannot bear to hear my word. You are of your father the devil, and your will is to do your father's desires. He was a murderer from the beginning, and does not stand in the truth, because there is no truth in him. When he lies, he speaks out of his own character, for he is a liar and the father of lies. But because I tell the truth, you do not believe me.[6]*

The afore-mentioned, doctrine of cessationism is a definite means of dream devaluation. Try selling that one to the following men who came along in the 1800s, far later than the first-century Church:

Myconius' Dream:
When Martin Luther set out on the work which shook the world, his friend Myconius expressed sympathy. "But," he said, "I can best help where I am. I will remain and pray while you toil." Myconius prayed day by day, but as he prayed he began to feel uncomfortable.

Mysteries in the Night

One night he had a dream. He thought the Saviour himself approached and showed him his hands and feet. He saw the fountain in which he had been cleansed from sin. Then looking earnestly into his eyes the Saviour said, "Follow me." The Lord took him to a lofty mountain and pointed eastward. Looking in that direction Myconius saw a plain stretching away to the horizon. It was dotted with white sheep—thousands and thousands of them. One man was trying to shepherd them all. The man was Luther. The Saviour pointed westward. Myconius saw a great field of standing corn. One reaper was trying to harvest it all. The lonely laborer was spent and exhausted, but still he persisted in his task. Myconius recognized in the solitary reaper his old friend Luther.

"It is not enough," said Myconius when he awakened, "that I should pray. The sheep must be shepherded; the fields must be reaped. Here am I; send me." And he went out and shared his old friend's labors.[7]

Alexander Duff's Dream:
A Scottish boy, lying on the heather beside a brook, fell asleep and had a wonderful dream. The sky became glorious with a dazzling golden light. Out of this light came a chariot drawn by horses of fire. Faster and faster it came down from the sky, and when it came near the boy he heard a voice as sweet as the mountain brook, saying, "Come up hither, I

have work for thee to do." When he got up to obey, he awoke, and found it was a dream.

The impression did not leave him, and one day the boy went to his room, knelt down beside the bed, and prayed, "O Lord, Thou knowest that silver and gold I have none. What I have I give to Thee. I offer myself. Wilt Thou accept the gift?" God did accept the gift, and that boy became one of the truly great missionaries.[8]

Both of these men were living proof that God still uses dreams, or at least He did during the Age of Enlightenment. Can you even imagine that the enemy would have inspired either of them to be greater ambassadors for Christ? Not hardly! But if they are too far back, how about the dreams of people you might recognize who are alive and well right now?

Rob Gross is the senior pastor of Mountain View Community Church (MVCC), Kaneohe, Hawaii:

In 1997, the Lord showed me in a dream a large airplane-shaped training center that would equip God's people for supernatural works of ministry. Later that year, John Eckhardt from Crusader's Ministry in Chicago prophesied at Grace Bible Church over my wife, Barbara, and I that God was going to release the finances we needed to fulfill what He was calling us to do.

Paul Cox is the co-founder of Aslan's Place in Apple Valley CA. Also, along with his wife, Donna, and Rob and Barb Gross, are co-founders of the Kingdom Institute. Paul recalls a dream from October 2004:

> I was in a large warehouse like building like Costco, but I thought, "This is like Walmart." The warehouse was huge, and there were large boxes everywhere; they were like ship containers; but smaller, perhaps like airplane cargo bins. I looked up and they were stacked very high, at least 10-plus stories up. There were so many we could barely walk through the aisles. I was very frustrated and said, "How can I do a seminar with all these boxes." No one will be able to see me. I then heard the word, "Provision."
>
> There was much activity and a stage area was cleared; People were everywhere, including a lot of youth. I recognized the son of a Hawaiian pastor, and I had a sense of about 250 people, but the numbers kept growing. The audience was growing so fast, it was out of control. The youth were especially active; so many that I had difficulty getting their attention. I looked behind me and another group was coming in, led by the son of my pastor friend.

For years, Paul and others kept their eyes open for that warehouse. In 2010, Aslan's Place was illegally forced by the city to either operate underground or relocate. On occasion,

A Fresh Perspective on Dreams

they shared a commercial space with anther church. Was that it? No. Later, an actual warehouse became avail able to rent. Was that it? Again, no. Finally, in 2011, the Lord was gracious to provide a new home for Aslan's Place in Apple Valley; it was a single-family dwelling, a far cry from a warehouse, but God hadn't forgotten the dreams of either Rob or Paul.

Little did Rob know that the Lord would eventually fulfill Eckhardt's prophetic word, but it would be 25 years later. MVCC had continued to meet in an elementary school cafeteria throughout most of that time, until Covid forced them to find worship alternatives such as broadcasting services from a home. But in 2022, after a series of miraculous interventions by God, the church finally took ownership of a very large commercial building where they currently meet and are in the process of remodeling.[9]

During the purchase process, Rob invited Paul and Donna to come to Hawaii and see the building. As soon as Paul walked in, he recognized the warehouse as the one he'd seen in his dream. A bit later, he also realized that the pastor's son in his 2004 dream was now an adult who has taken over for his dad as their church's pastor; and he was in attendance at one of the first meetings at the new building. As things have developed, an influx of on-fire-for-God millennials are flooding MVCC. Can there be any doubt that Rob's and Paul's prophetic dreams were not of God? Can there be any doubt that God could see well into the future and those dreams were meant to prepare both Rob and Paul for what was yet to come? Can there be any doubt that He will use the whole thing for His glory? The answer to all three questions is a resounding, "No!" Conversely, is there any conceivable way that the enemy planted those dreams, that they were only wishful thinking, or that they were lies? Not hardly!!!

The truth is, God has never stopped speaking through dreams, to both believers and un-believers just as He did throughout the Bible:

> *Jesus Christ is the same yesterday and today and forever.*[10]

> *Do not be deceived, my beloved brothers. Every good gift and every perfect gift is from above, coming down from the Father of lights, with whom there is no variation or shadow due to change.*[11]

Regardless of why the importance of our dreams has been diminished, we'd do well to adopt the use-it-or-lose it principle instead of relegating dreams to the trash like we might do with old news:

> It was once thought that any brain function lost was irretrievable. Today, research into what's referred to as "brain plasticity" has proven that this is not the case. On the contrary, your brain continues to make new neurons throughout life in response to mental activity.

> The inherent plasticity of the brain was discovered some 30 years ago, and not long thereafter, animal

models demonstrated that brain deterioration and aging were in fact reversible, provided the appropriate brain engagement.

The basic concept is simple. The brain changes physically, functionally, and chemically, as you acquire any ability or skill. You know this instinctively. Something must be changing as your abilities improve, or as new abilities emerge. You are actually remodeling your brain machinery by 'practicing' the skill; those physical changes account for your learning.[12]

Believe it or not, use-it-or-lose-it is actually a biblical principle. In Jesus' parable of the talents, just consider the talents/money to be dreams and the conclusion becomes obvious:

He also who had received the one talent came forward, saying, 'Master, I knew you to be a hard man, reaping where you did not sow, and gathering where you scattered no seed, so I was afraid, and I went and hid your talent in the ground. Here, you have what is yours.' But his master answered him, 'You wicked and slothful servant! You knew that I reap where I have not sown and gather where I scattered no seed? Then you ought to have invested my money with the bankers, and at my coming I should have received what was my own with interest. So take the talent from him and give it to him who has the ten talents. <u>For to everyone who has will more be given, and he will have an abundance. But from the one who has not, even what he has will be taken away.</u>[13]

Let's not be like that wicked and slothful servant and allow our dreams to be taken away.

---

[1] https://www.quora.com/What-is-the-region-of-money-devaluation?share=1

[2] John 10:10

[3] *The New International Version* (Grand Rapids, MI: Zondervan, 2011), Proverbs 12:13–14.

[4] Matthew 12:36-37

[5] Psalm 19:14

[6] John 8:43-45

[7] Tan, P. L. (1996). *Encyclopedia of 7700 Illustrations: Signs of the Times* (p. 1054). Garland, TX: Bible Communications, Inc.

[8] Ibid, 816-817

[9] MVCC's miracle story can found in *The Revelation of the Vault*

[10] Hebrews 13:8

[11] James 1:16-17

[12] https://www.brainhq.com/news/use-it-or-lose-it-the-principles-of-brain-plasticity/

[13] Matthew 25:24-29

Chapter Three:
Old Dreams Made New

Writing this book in tandem with researching and preparing a curriculum for a future course on dreams, I was astounded by some of the things of which I was reminded while reviewing my own old dreams. It shouldn't have been a surprise because it has become clear throughout the *Exploring Heavenly Places* series, that the Holy Spirit is constantly taking us back to things we thought we knew; which in retrospect were only a foundation for what the Lord wants to teach us now. So, in the hope that my readers will be encouraged to re-visit their own dreams, I'd like to share how a few of mine have either been fulfilled or become relevant in new ways over the years.

Waiting on the Lord:
How many of us have had dreams years ago that we've never fully understood? I would hazard a guess that would include most people. As I share how the Lord has spoken to me through long-distant dreams, I pray He will light a spark upon the old dreams of others, causing them to blaze to life anew in order to reveal His mysteries; His promises.

Among biblical dreamers, Joseph is among the most famous, and many lessons can be learned from his experience, but for the purpose of this particular chapter, let's look at Him as second-only-to-Pharoah in Egypt:

> *Now Joseph was governor over the land. He was the one who sold to all the people of the land. And Joseph's brothers came and bowed themselves before him with their faces to the ground. Joseph saw his brothers and recognized them, but he treated them like strangers and spoke roughly to them. "Where do you come from?" he said. They said, "From the land of Canaan, to buy food." And Joseph recognized his brothers, but they did not recognize him. And Joseph remembered the dreams that he had dreamed of them. And he said to them, "You are spies; you have come to see the nakedness of the land."*[1]

Joseph had been just seventeen years old when his jealous brothers sold him into slavery, not long after he shared two dreams in which they all were bowing down to him. Now, he was close to forty, so about twenty-three years had passed. We have no knowledge of how often Joseph must have thought about those early dreams, wondering, "What was that all about?" But, God hadn't forgotten and was at work in Joseph's life in the interim; like the potter with the clay, fashioning him into the man who made it possible for all of Israel to survive. I imagine though, while outwardly playing his part as a stern governor and still concealing his identity from his brothers, inwardly he was praising God with a joyful heart. Apparently, God had quite the family reunion planned all along, but it just wasn't time for the dreams to be fulfilled yet. His timing is oh-so-important, not just in everyday events but in seeing the fulfillment of dreams, sometimes immediate and other times over a few weeks, months or years; or, like Joseph, Rob Gross and Paul Cox, over many years.

> *For everything there is a season, and a time for every matter under heaven...He has made everything beautiful in its time. Also, he has put eternity into man's heart, yet so that he cannot find out what God has done from the beginning to the end.*[2]

> *The secret things belong to the LORD our God, but the things that are revealed belong to us and to our children forever, that we may do all the words of this law.*[3]

Sometimes all we can do is wait in faith to see how our dreams may eventually play out:

> *Now faith is the assurance of things hoped for, the conviction of things not seen. For by it the people of old received their commendation. By faith we understand that the universe was created by the word of God, so that what is seen was not made out of things that are visible.*

Joseph-like Time-delayed Dreams:
Recently, I spoke with a lady who is entering into a new season in her life. Toward the end of our conversation about all the exciting things that are happening, she said that she had one dream from sixteen years ago that she'd never understood. She began describing that dream, and I immediately knew it was a calling dream that is now reaching fulfillment in her new season. The interpretation resonated with her and she was filled with joy.

Mysteries in the Night

Many of us can pinpoint such a moment in time when the Lord spoke clearly to our heart in one way or another about His plan for our lives. For me, that happened when I was twelve years old at a youth retreat when I encountered the Holy Spirit as I never had before. In retrospect, I understand that's when I was first baptized by the Spirit, though it'd been about five years since I became a Christian; and it would be a very, very long time before I began understanding the things of the Spirit. In that moment though, I knew that I knew that I knew that the Lord was calling me into fulltime Christian service; but I made a big rookie mistake and immediately adopted some incorrect assumptions.

I had known from my earliest memory, at around three years old, that I was going to be a nurse when I grew up; so now, if I was going into fulltime service for God, I would undoubtedly become a foreign missionary, probably to Africa. Clearly, I hadn't yet learned that God rarely accomplishes things exactly the way we expect! Of course, nothing happened the way I thought it would, and I spent 40 years wondering what that call on my life was all about. Did I make a mistake? How could I have been so wrong about such an amazing experience?

Then in May 2003, approximately forty years later, I had a dream that really bothered me because neither could I understand it nor get it out of my mind. I'd started journaling a few years before, but was still brand new to the concept of dreams being important. From my journal:

A Fresh Perspective on Dreams

Lord, I had a dream and it remains in my mind. I've asked you to remove the memory of it unless you have something to teach me; but I still remember it so I'm going to write it down and then you can use it as you like — or not.

I was in a room with other people, though I don't remember exactly how many. There were some small windows along one wall, and at the end of the room a big picture window with a window shade. Quite unexpectedly, it started to snow outside and everyone was pretty excited. The others were looking out the smaller windows, but I was the only one who thought to raise the shade and look out of the big window.

Then it started snowing really hard, and for some reason the others left the room, except for one other person somewhere in the background. I can't remember who it was, or even exactly when I knew the person was there. The snow was coming down so hard that it not only covered everything around us outside in just a few minutes, but it was deepening by several inches in less than a minute. The snow level was rising so fast that it would soon have covered the building. I suddenly knew it was evil, rebuked Satan, and immediately the snow stopped. My first reaction was fear of his power, but also awe at the ability I'd had to tell him to stop. I wasn't comfortable with what had happened because it was so big and scary; but right away I knew I didn't have to be afraid because of You, Lord.

I, or possibly we, left the room and went into another part of the building. It was large and open, with lots of windows; and it was bright and sunny and green outside. There was no snow at all except a little around the foundation, but it quickly tapered off to green grass and I knew that the rest would soon melt away and be gone.

I seldom remember dreams, and I asked You to allow this one to fade because it seemed so disturbing, but I still remember. I've never had any dream messages or visions from You, at least none that I've recognized, so I'm not going to worry or dwell on this any longer. If You have something there for me to see, I'm willing for You to show me, and I'll listen for Your voice. If it's just me imagining, and trying to read something into it that's not there it'll just remain in these pages and be forgotten.

But it wasn't forgotten; it kept coming to mind time and again, but I didn't know why. Several years later, I came to Aslan's Place and began learning about recognizing evil and commanding it to leave in Jesus' name. Finally it clicked; I was to learn how to confront the enemy and send him on his way because God had given us that authority in and through His Son.

Then in December 2003, apparently God wanted to remind me of His call on my life, and I journaled:

> Good morning Father. I'm not sure exactly what I've been dreaming but I somehow have the sense that You are way too big for my dreams. There was something about various people, perhaps in the Old Testament, but there was something missing that would indicate your greatness. Then I woke up with a beautiful praise song in my head. I can't remember all the words, but it was something about You, the Almighty God, saying, "Whom shall I send?" And me replying, "Here I am Lord, send me."

Later, I wondered if the Old Testament reference was:

> *And I heard the voice of the Lord saying, "Whom shall I send, and who will go for us?" Then I said, "Here I am! Send me." And he said, "Go, and say to this people: 'Keep on hearing, but do not understand; keep on seeing, but do not perceive.' Make the heart of this people dull, and their ears heavy, and blind their eyes; lest they see with their eyes, and hear with their ears, and understand with their hearts, and turn and be healed."* [4]

But what about the fulltime part of my original calling? I was working part time as a hospice nurse, and saw no way to become a fulltime prayer minister. How could I reconcile my original calling, my career and my dream? I couldn't; because apparently the Lord wanted to be the one who planned the course of my life. He taught me that I was to be His fulltime emissary regardless of what I was currently doing in my life, so my dying patients became my mission field for a time. Meanwhile, I continued to travel back-and-forth as often as possible to Aslan's Place to soak up everything I could of the things of the Spirit, and to learn how to do generational prayer. Fast-forward to now, and that dream still has much to do with what has become my ministry, which varies from day to day depending on what the Lord has on His agenda for me. Whatever that may be, I am called to seek Him first, 100% of the time, whether I'm praying with someone, writing a book, fixing dinner or playing with my grandchildren - I'm His fulltime.

Symbolic, Prophetic or Both?
In reviewing my older dreams, this one from June 2016, shocked me:

> At a conference where it seems I had been before, There were several sets of books I'd written that had been placed on display for sale - big coffee-table sized books in full color. I think they were $20 each, but a man I seemed to know from North Carolina was talking to me about how much to charge. Only a few had ever been printed because of the cost; I didn't even have a copy so I took a set for myself. As I looked, someone else's name was on them as the author and I knew it was a donor who'd paid for the publication; yet my name wasn't there even though I'd written them. It had been a huge project that took several years. Finally, I found my name,

and it was as I now write as Barbara Kain Parker in very small print, engraved inside the cover at a margin. The engraved letters were white I think, or they might have been gold.

To give context, at this point I'd only written three books, most of which had been given away to friends and family. Paul Cox and I hadn't written the first volume of *Exploring Heavenly Places* yet (it was published in December 2016). I had no idea that by 2022, I would be writing this, the twelfth book I've either authored or co-authored since that dream. Additionally, I initially wrote those books simply as Barbara Parker and didn't begin using my maiden name, Kain, until a year or two later.

The one undeniable interpretation I had at the time was that with any books I write, the author and finisher is the Lord, for He is the one who both downloads all of the inspiration and revelation. (Trust me, you wouldn't want to read something I develop – it would be like reading a drier-than-dry, research paper.) How appropriate that my name was tiny in comparison to His, for He knows what I will think or speak or write, well before I do:

> *Even before a word is on my tongue, behold, O LORD, you know it altogether.*[5]

Thoughts and prayer from my journal:

> Could these books be the books of my life that have already been written, with You as my author and finisher? After all, You have already paid the price

for my life. Those words in white would indicate they are recorded in righteousness; or , if in gold, covered in Your glory.

Then I said, "Behold, I have come; in the scroll of the book it is written of me: I delight to do your will, O my God; your law is within my heart."[6]

Your eyes saw my unformed substance; in your book were written, every one of them, the days that were formed for me, when as yet there was none of them.[7]

Looking back at this surprising dream now, my sense is that there may be more to come; things that are prophetic about coming books I may write. Time will tell and I will wait and watch:

I wait for the LORD, *my soul waits, and in his word I hope; my soul waits for the Lord more than watchmen for the morning, more than watchmen for the morning.*[8]

Repeated Warning, Blessing or Both?
The following instances exemplify again how the Lord always knows well in advance what is coming our way.

In June 2003, my husband and I were volunteers at a deliverance ministry when I had very similar dreams two days in a row:

I was driving a car when a woman who was driving ahead of me was, somehow, now behind me. She was talking on a cell phone, and I knew it was with her husband and she was asking for instructions. When or how she got behind me, I'm not sure; but somehow she was suddenly coming through the back window, and I knew she was not nice - she was trying to harm me. I was enveloped in total blackness for a few seconds before I woke up, but even though it was kind of scary, my waking thought that I was ok because God was with me. Then there was a bit of fear of the unknown, but briefly, because God gave me comfort and peace.

This is the second morning in a row, when I went back to sleep, but then woke up with a start due to a sort-of-scary dream. Today, driving pretty fast, I had just gone through an intersection when the windshield fogged up; even worse, it was a thick, icy cover and the wipers wouldn't get rid of it. I tried to brush it away on the inside, praying frantically while driving; I couldn't see the lines on the road, or anything else for that matter, but I didn't wreck or go off course at all. Then the windshield started to clear and I could again see where I was going.

A year later, it became apparent that a lady who was part of the ministry and who was supposed to be my mentor, was actually very destructive to both my husband and me. He wanted to walk away, which I would have loved to do, except that we'd made a 3-month commitment for me to work in that office. On top of that, the Lord had also given me a dream that made it clear I was exactly where I was supposed to be. At some point, I realized that the two dreams above meant that this woman would be very destructive, putting me in extreme danger both emotionally and spiritually, trying to run my ministry off the road. As I endured her abuse, there was comfort in knowing that the Lord had my back; and in retrospect, I came to understand that the Lord had been training me for what was to come. We finally left, totally burnt out, and I didn't want to ever again have anything to do with any deliverance ministry, but my husband, who is really gifted in knowing the next place we need to go, found Aslan's Place online and suggested we go to a school there. Apparently, this guy (Paul Cox) had all these sensations on his head, so maybe we could find out what was wrong with me. You see, my discernment had been activated during the traumatic time we'd just come through, but at the time we had zero knowledge of what discernment is. So we went, and by the time we finished the first day, I knew I'd come home. It wasn't long before I began realized that I had not only already learned the hard way what <u>not</u> to do, but had also experienced first-hand what it meant to be around someone with Dissociative Identity Disorder; someone who could be sweet and encouraging one day and totally abusive the next, or who might switch personalities from moment to moment.

On another occasion in 2003, I had a dream in which there was a large, steep hill in front of me. It was covered with footprints that I knew were mine, and I heard the Lord tell me I had to climb up the hill once more, but that this time it wouldn't be as hard as previous trips up that grade. I wasn't happy because the hill represented a very difficult personal situation, but of course He was right. Within 24 hours, the same problem came up again and it was much easier and quickly handled. After the fact, I was again grateful for His heads-up because I wasn't as overcome with angst that I had to do this again; and the unwelcome dream became a blessing.

Our Lord knows well ahead of time what we need, so we never have to succumb to fear:

> *You hem me in, behind and before, and lay your hand upon me. Such knowledge is too wonderful for me; it is high; I cannot attain it.*[9]

Summary:
Speaking with a good friend, we were talking about how amazing it is that Rob's dream from 1997 (recounted in chapter two) is only now being realized in 2022; not only that, but it intersects with the fulfillment of Paul's dream from 2004. We ended up reviewing one of her old dreams that she's never understood, and Lord revealed that it was a directional dream for this moment in her life.

Think about your own dreams. Do you have one (or more) that you've never forgotten or completely understood? If so, consider revisiting and praying into it; first to find out what the Lord may want to reveal. Then, if it is still 'as clear as mud', get help from someone who understands a little more

Mysteries in the Night

about dream interpretation; and keep at it until you get some clarity.

How blessed it is when things the Lord spoke long ago in dreams:

- Are realized as having come to fruition; proof that God's means what He says and keeps His promises

- Spark a memory of a warning/blessing scenario that reminds us of His steadfast love and faithfulness and delivers a new sense of hope for a current trial

- Fresh dream interpretations that are only clear in retrospect; reminders that He always goes both before and behind us

Consider God's words to Isaiah:

Thus says the LORD, *who makes a way in the sea, a path in the mighty waters, who brings forth chariot and horse, army and warrior; they lie down, they cannot rise, they are extinguished, quenched like a wick: "Remember not the former things, nor consider the things of old. Behold, I am doing a new thing; now it springs forth, do you not perceive it? I will make a way in the wilderness and rivers in the desert.*[10]

In reviewing our old dreams we may well discover that He is indeed doing a new thing in/through us!

A Fresh Perspective on Dreams

[1] Genesis 42:6-9a
[2] Ecclesiastes 3:1, 11
[3] Deuteronomy 29:29
[4] Isaiah 6:8-10
[5] Psalm 139:4
[6] Psalm 40:7-8
[7] Psalm 139:16
[8] Psalm 130:5-6
[9] Psalm 139:5-6
[10] Isaiah 43:16-19a

Mysteries in the Night

Chapter Four:
CLUES & LIFE

Have you ever played *Clue?* For anyone who hasn't, it's the classic murder mystery board game in which players ask questions using the process of elimination to weed out suspects, weapons and rooms in which the crime may have been committed. Ultimately, the winner will have identified the murderer after sifting through multiple possibilities. But how does that apply to dreams? A dream may be either quickly understood or very obscure and difficult to unravel; but if it's from God, there is an answer because:

> *It is the glory of God to conceal things, but the glory of kings is to search things out.*[1]

Often our dreams are mysteries, and sometimes a variety of clues are needed to solve them. It's a well-established fact that that the Lord often uses that which is familiar to speak to us in dreams; and the people, places, events and objects in our dreams have meanings that are unique to the individual. But sometimes it takes some creative processing, pondering and praying to put seemingly unrelated things together, going so far as to connect that which happens during sleep to both a twilight experience and every-day life.

Let me illustrate how an such intersection of waking and sleeping occurred for me, with the hope that my experience may get your own interpretive juices flowing.

Mysteries in the Night

I have always loved four-part harmony! Growing up in church and throughout many years as an adult, I sang in church choirs and loved participating in or listening to gospel quartets. Christmas performances were especially joyful, with favorites ranging from *Silent Night* to the *Hallelujah Chorus*. Then, looking for something new to help fill my empty nest after our son went off to college, I joined a Sweet Adelines barbershop chorus, which only enhanced my love of harmony.

Sweet Adelines regularly compete amongst themselves in both quartet and choral competitions, always striving to get every aspect of a tune exactly right—word perfect, note perfect, timing perfect. At times, the blend of voices singing four different notes is so precise, and comes together in such unity, that the music literally sends shivers down your spine. Every once in a while we would hit that perfect chord and produce a unique sound called an overtone in which a fifth note, sometimes called a fifth voice, is clearly heard. When this occurred it we would find ourselves standing in silence afterward; awestruck by the beauty of the harmony, with emotional tears flooding our eyes and hairs on our arms standing straight up.

Since leaving the chorus, I continue to listen on occasion to the music of several championship quartets because, in case it wasn't clear before, I absolutely love harmony!

The Lord often sings to me; it can be anything from a phrase to a whole song; it can be oldies, popular music, worship tunes – pretty much anything I've heard before, even if it's been years ago. In the following scenario I hadn't been listening to any barbershop music recently so the music wasn't already going around endlessly in my mind like tunes tend to do (especially disliked commercial jingles!). From my journal:

> I awoke with the *Tennessee Waltz* playing in my head. My first thought was, "Why?" because it's a song about lost love; about how a friend stole a lover away. But, Jesus, my lover who sings to me, could not be stolen by anyone; so what was this all about? As I pondered it, I realized that the version I was hearing was a barbershop recording in which there is one phrase that includes a chord that is so very precise that it gives me chills. It's so perfect that I often replay just the one phrase over and over again just to soak in the harmony of "Remember, remember the night," with 'night' being the word that resonates all the way down to my toes. As I thought about it, that phrase was all I'd been hearing; not the whole song with its sad tale of woe.

On the particular night in question, I had gone to sleep not feeling very well; but as I laid my head on the pillow I told the Lord I really wanted to rest, but that in my rest I also wanted to go anywhere and do anything He wanted to do with me. The next morning I awoke knowing that I had dreamed a lot, but couldn't recall what had happened except that there had been one dream in which there were a lot of little yellow snakes that were being dealt with. My sense was that I had been cooperating with God to deal with curses that had come against me in order to rob me of hope (snakes being curses and yellow often representing hope in my dreams). Now, if there's anything that I hate it is snakes; so any dream that includes them always gets my attention! I really, really needed some confirmation they'd been dealt with. Suddenly, I remembered God's twilight[2] serenade, and I understood:

> I realize that there are two messages here for me this morning. First, there is perfect harmony when I am in unity with God (actually, me + Father + Jesus + Holy Spirit = a quartet!), even in times of trouble. Second, "Remember the night," or in other words, remember the dreams of last night. It's about the moments of perfect harmony that occurred during the night when my spirit interacted in unity - in perfect harmony - with God.

There was no doubt in my mind, the snakes were gone; and no simple dream-interpretation formula could have given me that assurance. It only came through journaling and prayer, when the Lord put seemingly isolated pieces together; His serenade + its meaning in my life + my dreams = comforting assurances direct from His heart to mine. In essence, He used things I love (harmony and unity with Him) to overcome things I hate with a passion (snakes and evil).

There's another game called *The Game of Life*, which simulates an individual's journey through life; beginning in early childhood and progressing all the way through to retirement. Along the way, events such as college, jobs, marriage and having children are tossed into the mix. This game is a good illustration of how each life offers lots of clues; none of which can be discounted when deciphering how our dreams intersect with our everyday reality.

---

[1] Proverbs 25:2

[2] The 'twilight' time is that which occurs on the verge of waking; it's a time in which one is connected to both the spiritual and physical realms in such a way that things that are seen or heard are generally very important

Mysteries in the Night

Chapter Five
Dream Killers in Disguise

Almost any good mystery novel or spy movie has one or more killers on the loose, and the hero or heroine needs to figure out 'who done it' in order to restore order and deliver justice. If this chapter were such a book or screenplay, the plot would quickly become very complex because in the case of dreams, the 'killers' are many.

From the easiest to explain (i.e., loud noises or indigestion) to the most difficult to tackle (i.e., health issues or generational iniquity), the enemy will use all the tools in his belt to detract from righteous dreams. The one with whom we do battle over our dreams is clear:

> *For we do not wrestle against flesh and blood, but against the rulers, against the authorities, against the cosmic powers over this present darkness, against the spiritual forces of evil in the heavenly places.*[1]

Some of the worst offenders don't even make it to the usual lists of dream blockers, but they should:

Attitudes:
When such things as anger, worry, bitterness or grief consume us, we become trapped in the ungodly dimensions where we are unable to clearly hear and process God's voice. In such places, our dreams may seem to be either absent or tormented. Sometimes, professional help is

needed, and may include either medical/psychiatric care or generational deliverance; but often, the solution is as simple as choosing to align an attitude to God's Word:

> *Therefore, since Christ suffered in his body, <u>arm yourselves also with the same attitude</u>, because whoever suffers in the body is done with sin.*[2]
>
> *Do not be conformed to this world, <u>but be transformed by the renewal of your mind</u>, that by testing you may discern what is the will of God, what is good and acceptable and perfect.*[3]

Stinking Thinking:
Such seemingly insignificant things as the negative news of the day, an overly busy calendar, a demanding job or other responsibilities can detract from a healthy dream life. In those cases, the solution is akin to that regarding bad attitudes:

> *We destroy arguments and every lofty opinion raised against the knowledge of God, and <u>take every thought captive to obey Christ</u>...*[4]

Sinful Behaviors:
Remember Saul? His disobedience was sin, and it killed his ability to hear from God. He learned the hard way that sin is a definite dream killer, and his experience gives biblical precedence that being rebellious against God can and will impact our ability to hear from Him.

Consider Nebuchadnezzar; he was quite the dreamer, even before he became a believer in the one true God. He had a dream that Daniel interpreted, which warned him of dire consequences if he didn't repent, but Nebuchadnezzar's pride was so great that he didn't heed the warning. The words Daniel later spoke to his successor, Belshazzar, should cause the fear of the Lord to resonate in our hearts today:

> *O king, the Most High God gave Nebuchadnezzar your father kingship and greatness and glory and majesty. And because of the greatness that he gave him, all peoples, nations, and languages trembled and feared before him. Whom he would, he killed, and whom he would, he kept alive; whom he would, he raised up, and whom he would, he humbled. But when his heart was lifted up and his spirit was hardened so that he dealt proudly, he was brought down from his kingly throne, and his glory was taken from him. He was driven from among the children of mankind, and his mind was made like that of a beast, and his dwelling was with the wild donkeys. He was fed grass like an ox, and his body was wet with the dew of heaven, until he knew that the Most High God rules the kingdom of mankind and sets over it whom he will.*[5]

Ultimately, everything happened exactly as predicted, because the king didn't understand the consequences of pride:

When pride comes, then comes disgrace, but with the humble is wisdom.[6]

Pride goes before destruction, and a haughty spirit before a fall.[7]

Before destruction a man's heart is haughty, but humility comes before honor.[8]

If Nebuchadnezzar even dreamed during the time he lived as a beast in the fields, his madness would have precluded his ability to hear God clearly or process those dreams. The sin of pride could also easily interfere with our ability to hear His voice as well.

Consistently choosing sin over obedience is a sure-fire way to lose the ability to hear from the Lord, whether in dreams or by any other means. Jesus illustrated this truth when He quoted Isaiah:

"He has blinded their eyes and hardened their heart, lest they see with their eyes, and understand with their heart, and turn, and I would heal them."[9]

Could there be a rebound effect if we harm someone else's sleep? For good or bad, our sinful actions always have consequences so, in the following example, what if instead of a receiving a blessing for returning a poor man's cloak, you choose to keep it? Might the poor man then retaliate by cursing your sleep? It's certainly possible.

You shall stand outside, and the man to whom you make the loan shall bring the pledge out to you. And if he is a poor man, you shall not sleep in his pledge. You shall restore to him the pledge as the sun sets, that he may sleep in his cloak and bless you. And it shall be righteousness for you before the Lord your God.[10]

Since the list of infractions against others is endless, we would do well to heed Jesus' words if we'd like to have a good night's sleep that is blessed with righteous dreams:

So whatever you wish that others would do to you, do also to them, for this is the Law and the Prophets.[11]

Fear:

Fear is a huge component of false dreams, night terrors, etc. No wonder the enemy harasses kids; no wonder bad dreams are such a huge part of PTSD; no wonder Job was so desperate:

For the thing that I fear comes upon me, and what I dread befalls me. Am not at ease, nor am I quiet; I have no rest, but trouble comes.[12]

Contrast Job's complaint with King David's response when his son, Absalom, was seeking his life. His ability to trust God in the worst of circumstances paid huge dividends:

LORD, how many are my foes! How many rise up against me! Many are saying of me, "God will not deliver him." But you, LORD, are a shield around me, my glory, the One who lifts my head high. I call out to the LORD, and he answers me from his holy mountain. <u>I lie down and sleep; I wake again, because the LORD sustains me</u>. I will *not fear though tens of thousands assail me on every side.*[13]

The importance of believing and receiving God's promises is always critical to our well-being. That truth applies to a restful night's sleep, which is conducive to dreaming. Consider David's faith again:

> <u>*In peace I will both lie down and sleep*</u>; *for you alone, O Lord, make me dwell in safety.* [14]

Foolishness:

Folly and foolishness are inseparable:

> *Answer not a fool according to his folly, lest you be like him yourself. Answer a fool according to his folly, lest he be wise in his own eyes.*[15]

Folly, as described in Proverbs 9, is pretty much the exact opposite of wisdom. Therefore, neither foolishness nor folly are going to result in a good night's sleep, because that is promised in the presence of wisdom and discretion:

> *My son, do not lose sight of these – keep sound wisdom and discretion, and they will be life for your soul and adornment for your neck. Then you will walk on your way securely, and your foot will not stumble. If you lie down, you will not be afraid; when you lie down, your sleep will be sweet.*[16]

Greed:

This is a hidden dream killer that we may not have considered, but Scripture is clear:

> *When goods increase, they increase who eat them, and what advantage has their owner but to see them with his eyes? <u>Sweet is the sleep of a laborer, whether he eats little or much, but the full stomach of the rich will not let him sleep.</u>*[17]

Idolatry:
Scripture is also clear that idolatry disrupts our dreams and actually instigates false dreams.

> *For <u>the household gods utter nonsense, and the diviners see lies; they tell false dreams</u> and give empty consolation. Therefore the people wander like sheep; they are afflicted for lack of a shepherd.*[18]

Most Christians would quickly agree such worship of idols should be shunned. But, what do idols look like today? Or put another way, what addictions control and infect our dreams? It's common knowledge that alcohol and drugs affect our sleep and our dreams, but they are among the obvious culprits. Others are more obscure and include anything that one pursues with greater passion than they do the Lord; and that list is endless. How about the pursuit of happiness? Or, the pursuit of education, power, money, a spouse, retirement or ownership of a home, to name a few? God made it clear that we are to have no other gods before Him, so we'd be wise to examine ourselves and repent of anything we place on a higher pedestal than Him. When He is our #1, our entire life will be revolutionized, and our dreams will likely reflect the blessing of His presence.

Compromise:
It's interesting that Daniel, who was so gifted with dreams and their interpretation, invariably refused to compromise with the ways of the world. As a teenager who had been taken captive, brought to Babylon, and selected for service to King Nebuchadnezzar, he chose to stand firm in his faith:

> *But Daniel resolved that he would not defile himself with the king's food, or with the wine that he drank. Therefore he asked the chief of the eunuchs to allow him not to defile himself.*[19]

Had he simply 'gone along to get along' by eating the food he was instructed to consume; he would have violated God's dietary laws. Many years and several kings later, Daniel was a very old man:

> *Then this Daniel became distinguished above all the other high officials and satraps, because an excellent spirit was in him. And the king planned to set him over the whole kingdom. Then the high officials and the satraps sought to find a ground for complaint against Daniel with regard to the kingdom, but they could find no ground for complaint or any fault, because he was faithful, and no error or fault was found in him. Then these men said, "We shall not find any ground for complaint against this Daniel unless we find it in connection with the law of his God."*[20]

Longer story short, the bad guys hatched a devious scheme they were certain would bring about Daniel's death in a den of lions; but they hadn't counted on his refusal to compromise:

> *Then these men came by agreement and found Daniel making petition and plea before his God.*[21]

So, the den of lions it was, but:

> *Then, at break of day, the king arose and went in haste to the den of lions. As he came near to the den where Daniel was, he cried out in a tone of anguish. The king declared to Daniel, "O Daniel, servant of the living God, has your God, whom you serve continually, been able to deliver you from the lions?" Then Daniel said to the king, "O king, live forever! My God sent his angel and shut the lions' mouths, and they have not harmed me, because I was found blameless before him; and also before you, O king, I have done no harm."*[22]

It doesn't seem to be a stretch to think that Daniel's gift of dreams and dream interpretation was one of God's many blessings throughout his life because of his obedience.

God hates compromise, as Jesus made clear:

> *No one can serve two masters, for either he will hate the one and love the other, or he will be devoted to the one and despise the other.*[23]

Self-sufficiency:
We are often taught that our well-being is tied to 'looking out for number one'. We are taught to strive for the best jobs,

the nicest toys, connections to influential people, and the list goes on. But all of that is contrary to God's Word:

> *Unless the Lord builds the house, those who build it labor in vain. Unless the Lord watches over the city, the watchman stays awake in vain. <u>It is in vain that you rise up early and go late to rest, eating the bread of anxious toil; for he gives to his beloved sleep.</u>*[24]

Since sleep is definitely conducive to dreaming, learning to die to self and depend on God for all of our needs just might be a good idea too. The Apostle Paul understood this:

> *I know how to be brought low, and I know how to abound. In any and every circumstance, I have learned the secret of facing plenty and hunger, abundance and need. I can do all things through him who strengthens me…And my God will supply every need of yours according to his riches in glory in Christ Jesus.*[25]

A popular concept these days is self-determination theory, which is nothing but self-sufficiency by another name. People are encouraged to apply it to every area of their lives, contrary to biblical truth:

> *Not that we are sufficient in ourselves to claim anything as coming from us, but our sufficiency is from God.*[26]

> *But he said to me, "My grace is sufficient for you, for my power is made perfect in weakness." Therefore I will boast all the more gladly of my weaknesses, so that the power of Christ may rest upon me.*[27]

Self-sufficiency or self-determination is a cross-over category of dream killers: it is also idolatry of self, compromise, foolishness/folly, sinful attitudes, thinking and behavior . Tragically, it leads to deception as one tries to mix the enemy's lies with God's truth. How often have you heard people say that they define their own truth? It happens all the time, and since our topic is dreams, let's discuss what that might look like.

Picture this: an individual decides to define his own faith, so he mixes a bit of the Bible together with Buddhism, Islam and New Age beliefs. Then he has a dream and seeks to interpret it through the lens of his hodgepodge religion. Assuming it wasn't a false dream to begin with, the final interpretation would definitely be flawed, if not deadly. God's truth no more mixes with mankind's ideologies than vinegar or ammonia mix with chlorine to produce toxic vapors that may cause serious burns. God is very serious about this! We would do well to heed His warning to the church at Pergamum:

> *But I have a few things against you: you have some there who hold the teaching of Balaam, who taught Balak to put a stumbling block before the sons of Israel, so that they might eat food sacrificed to idols and practice sexual immorality. So also you have some who hold the teaching of the Nicolaitans. Therefore repent. If not, I will come to you soon and war against them with the sword of my mouth.*[28]

Rebellion:
One day while listening to a sermon a friend had preached; Isaiah 29 was mentioned. I realized that as much as I've loved, studied and written about dreams, this passage hasn't often been on my radar; yet it illustrates perfectly the emptiness and lack of satisfaction that results from rebellion, comparing it to a false dream. You see, the enemy takes advantage of whatever weaknesses he can exploit; whether physical or emotional; he carries them over into our sleep, trying to cause distress and alienate us from God:

> *And the multitude of all the nations that fight against Ariel, all that fight against her and her stronghold and distress her, shall be like a dream, a vision of the night. As when a hungry man dreams, and behold, he is eating, and awakes with his hunger not satisfied, or as when a thirsty man dreams, and behold, he is drinking, and awakes faint, with his thirst not quenched, so shall the multitude of all the nations be that fight against Mount Zion. Astonish yourselves and be astonished; blind yourselves and be blind! Be drunk, but not with wine; stagger, but not with strong drink! For the LORD has poured out upon you a spirit of deep sleep, and has closed your eyes (the prophets), and covered your heads (the seers). And the vision of all this has become to you like the words of a book that is sealed. When men give it to one who can read, saying, "Read this," he says, "I cannot, for it is sealed." And when they give the book to one who cannot read, saying, "Read this," he says, "I cannot read."*

The consequences of rebellion are harsh, not the least of which is that messages from the Lord are sealed; and that includes the inability to comprehend His dream messages.

Finally:

The list of dream killers is as endless as the sins, whether personal or generational, that have either compromised our ability to sleep, to hear God's voice in our dreams, or to interpret dreams correctly. We are left with a choice:

> *And if it is evil in your eyes to serve the LORD, choose this day whom you will serve, whether the gods your fathers served in the region beyond the River, or the gods of the Amorites in whose land you dwell. But as for me and my house, we will serve the LORD.[29]*

---

[1] Ephesians 6:12

[2] *The New International Version* (Grand Rapids, MI: Zondervan, 2011), 1 Pe 4:1.

[3] Romans 12:2

[4] 2 Corinthians 10:5

[5] Daniel 5:18-21

[6] Proverbs 11:2

[7] Proverbs 16:18

[8] Proverbs 18:12

[9] John 12:40

[10] Deuteronomy 24:11-13

[11] Matthew 7:12

[12] Job 3:25-26

Mysteries in the Night

[13] Psalm 3:1-6
[14] Psalm 4:8
[15] Proverbs 26:4-5
[16] Proverbs 21:21;23
[17] Ecclesiastes 5:11
[18] Zechariah 10:2
[19] Daniel 1:8
[20] Daniel 6:3-5
[21] Daniel 6:11
[22] Daniel 6:19-22
[23] Matthew 6:24
[24] Psalm 27:1-2:
[25] Philippians 4:12-13, 19
[26] 1 Corinthians 3:5
[27] 1 Corinthians 12:9
[28] Revelation 3:14-16
[29] Joshua 24:15

CHAPTER SIX:
TRUE OR FALSE?

True-or-false questions on an exam – some love them, some hate them. Personally, I'm not a fan because in my mind there are often too many shades of gray. I analyze each question, each word, wondering what vocabulary tricks might exist to trip me up. Are there tiny little prefixes, suffixes or pronouns that completely change the meaning of a sentence? What did the writer mean by using a particular word that could have an alternate meaning? Complicating the issue, today's culture seemingly tries to re-define everything; so on whose version of truth is any question based? The positive news is that there's a 50-50 chance of guessing the right answer, and that may work well if one really understands the subject at hand; but there's also that same chance of getting it wrong, which could result in a failing grade.

When it comes to our dreams, we can't afford to get it wrong! God is very serious about the misuse of dreams:

> *So do not listen to your prophets, your diviners, your dreamers, your fortune-tellers, or your sorcerers, who are saying to you, 'You shall not serve the king of Babylon.' For it is a lie that they are prophesying to you, with the result that you will be removed far from your land, and I will drive you out, and you will perish.*[1]

Whoa! For Judah, that meant going into Babylonian captivity for seventy years; and most of us don't have that much time left. Fortunately, when it comes to determining the veracity of our dreams, we have two reliable sources by which we can determine truth versus fiction; God, in the person of the Teacher who is the Holy Spirit, and the Word of God, the Bible.

Unlike any true-or-false test in an academic setting, the way we handle God's truth versus the enemy's lies is critical to the well-being of body, soul and spirit. This is why a solid biblical foundation on which to build our understanding is critical. Even within the Church, there are differing opinions regarding what is truth and what is not. Why else are so many denominational squabbles over doctrine? Such disunity creates chaos and confusion, which is not of God; and the ungodly influence of others can produce havoc in our lives. Whom should we believe? Surely, the audience of Paul and Barnabas in Iconium could relate:

> *Now at Iconium they entered together into the Jewish synagogue and spoke in such a way that a great number of both Jews and Greeks believed. But <u>the unbelieving Jews stirred up the Gentiles and poisoned their minds</u> against the brothers. So they remained for a long time, speaking boldly for the Lord, who bore witness to the word of his grace, granting signs and wonders to be done by their hands. But <u>the people of the city were divided;</u> some sided with the Jews and some with the apostles.*[2]

Fortunately, we have a reliable litmus test to discern God's truth; a beginner's guide both to the Christian life in general and, more specifically, to understanding our dreams:

> *Beloved, <u>do not believe every spirit, but test the spirits to see whether they are from God</u>, for many false prophets have gone out into the world. By this you know the Spirit of God: every spirit that confesses that Jesus Christ has come in the flesh is from God, and every spirit that does not confess Jesus is not from God. This is the spirit of the antichrist, which you heard was coming and now is in the world already. Little children, you are from God and have overcome them, for he who is in you is greater than he who is in the world. They are from the world; therefore they speak from the world, and the world listens to them.*[3]

Biblical principles regarding God's truth that are not usually associated with dream interpretation, are relevant nevertheless:

> *Behold, you delight in truth in the inward being, and you teach me wisdom in the secret heart.*[4]

> *And now, O Lord GOD, you are God, and your words are true...*[5]

> *But, as it is written, "What no eye has seen, nor ear heard, nor the heart of man imagined, what God has prepared for those who love him" — these things God has revealed to us through the Spirit. For the Spirit searches everything, even the depths of God. For who knows a person's thoughts except the spirit of that person, which*

is in him? So also no one comprehends the thoughts of God except the Spirit of God. Now we have received not the spirit of the world, but the Spirit who is from God, that we might understand the things freely given us by God. And we impart this in words not taught by human wisdom but taught by the Spirit, interpreting spiritual truths to those who are spiritual.[6]

Let your steadfast love come to me, O LORD, your salvation according to your promise; then shall I have an answer for him who taunts me, for I trust in your word. And take not the word of truth utterly out of my mouth, for my hope is in your rules.[7]

Your word is a lamp to my feet and a light to my path.[8]

Our God-given dreams will <u>always</u> align with His Word; and His voice <u>always</u> trumps that of any other person or spiritual being.

John Knox was a Scottish minister and writer in the 1500s, as well as a leader of that country's reformation and the founder of the Presbyterian Church of Scotland. He had a dream that illustrated this truth:

> During his last hours, John Knox woke from a slumber sighing, and told his friends that he had just been tempted to believe that he had, "merited Heaven and eternal blessedness, by the faithful discharge of my ministry. But blessed be God who has enabled me to beat down and quench the fiery dart, by suggesting to me such passages of

> Scripture as this: *What hast thou that thou didst not receive?*[9] *By the grace of God I am what I am. Not I, but the grace of God which was with me.*[10]" [11]

As a young adult, Hal Lindsey's *Late, Great Planet Earth* was very popular, and the possibility of an imminent rapture was foremost in many of our minds. I often experienced false dreams about it; dreams in which I would suddenly find myself, along with many others, floating up into the sky. But it didn't take long to realize it wasn't really happening, the main reason being that it was a slow process; definitely not:

> ... *in a moment, in the twinkling of an eye, at the last trumpet.*[12]

I'm grateful that though I had no real understanding of the importance of dreams and dream interpretation at the time, I was well grounded enough in the Bible to know when I was dreaming about a lie.

Previously written in *Exploring Heavenly Places, Volume 8, Dreamspeak:*

> False dreams...can be realized as such, simply because a false doctrine that skews a biblical truth is recognized. Satan is clearly presented as an outright liar throughout scripture,[13] so we must know what the Bible actually says and not just what someone has told us it says in order to keep from being deceived in a dream. We may awake unsure or even distressed about a dream but when things

don't line up with what is known to be true, it can usually be dismissed as false. Alternatively, as one becomes more skilled in discernment they may be able to ask the Lord and then physically discern whether it is good or evil.

It seems very clear that the more we hide the Word of God in our hearts[14] and seek an intimate relationship with Him, the less likely we are to be led astray by false dreams.

With apologies to Shakespeare, "To be or not to be?" is not the question. Rather, it's, "True or false?" We get to choose to believe God's truth or the enemy's lies, and that choice is oh-so-critical when it applies to our dreams.

---

[1] Jeremiah 27:9-10

[2] Acts 14:1-4

[3] 1 John 4:1-5

[4] Psalm 51:6

[5] 2 Samuel 7:28a

[6] 1 Corinthians 2:9-13

[7] Psalm 119:41-43

[8] Psalm 119:105

[9] 1 Corinthians 4:7

[10] 1 Corinthians 15:10

[11] Tan, P. L. (1996). *Encyclopedia of 7700 Illustrations: Signs of the Times* (p. 529). Garland, TX: Bible Communications, Inc.

[12] 1 Corinthians 15:52a
[13] Genesis 3:4; John 8:44,
[14] Psalm 119:11

Mysteries in the Night

A Fresh Perspective on Dreams

Chapter Seven:
Dream Hackers

Our interest in false dreams was sparked anew during an Aslan's Place academy in March 2019. I had begun teaching about dreams, but had decided beforehand to share a dream that Paul had shown me earlier so the class could interpret it together. He'd received it the previous day from one of his friends in Singapore:

> I was having a nap on Monday afternoon. I had a dream and I felt I was sleeping in another dimension. Suddenly, I felt that I was shot with electricity. It was running all over my head. I saw a brown bottle and on it was written DH Heaton.

The lady had begun to work on the dream interpretation and had discovered:

- DH stands for 'dream hack'

- DH Heaton is a Swedish production company specializing in eSports tournaments and other gaming conventions

- Heaton is actually 'heat on', and is about gaming

So our journey into dream hacking began; first with a discernment from Paul, and then with various other participants (unidentified here except for Jana Green[1]) chiming in with their thoughts:

Paul discerned ungodly rulers and asked, "Is there a division of rulers that construct dreams? And, why do we get bad dreams?" Then he discerned something like a tentacle that was coming down from the ungodly heavens to each person.

I see the color red.

Jana: it's a strategy of an apostolic level, accessing the marketplace through us

I see an ungodly tree trunk, like hollow metal with hollow branches sticking out.

I'm seeing electrical towers that look like trees.

Paul discerned ungodly, dimensional rulers and thrones.

It looks like an ungodly root coming down to all of us.

Is this mind control?

Like an octopus—is it mind control, like an evil operator at a subconscious level?

A water spirit?

Jana: A spirit of counsel?

I'm hearing a high-pitched sound.

My feet just got very cold, like in snow two feet deep.

A Fresh Perspective on Dreams

There's a lack of fear of the Lord in this place!

Paul: We are all connected to this system.

It is tied to the night.

Paul: What if there is one Mazzaroth[2] that is in charge of day, and one of the night? Is ancient evil using dreams to connect with esoteric knowledge? Is it tied to Nimrod? (After a prayer for wisdom, counsel and understanding Paul discerned we were in a better place.)

Job had troublesome dreams and visions of the night:

> *In a dream, in a vision of the night, when deep sleep falls on men, while they slumber on their beds, then he opens the ears of men and terrifies them with warnings, that he may turn man aside from his deed and conceal pride from a man; he keeps back his soul from the pit, his life from perishing by the sword. "Man is also rebuked with pain on his bed and with continual strife in his bones, so that his life loathes bread, and his appetite the choicest food.[3]*

Paul: There were also dreams of straw in Jeremiah,[4] but what does it mean to prophesy lying dreams?[5] It's about people who prophesy false dreams that are taken as truth. Consider that in Jude 1:8, it speaks of people relying on their dreams and reviling glorious ones; Isaiah 56:10 says that His watchmen are blind and dreamers love to slumber; and, Jeremiah 27:9 says not to listen to your prophets, diviners, dreams, fortune tellers or sorcerers.

Jana received a scroll, which she read:

> Again, it is the alignment to the system of Babylon where vain imagination was given a reality. The sons of men knew no truth except by a false hope without proof. Everything was given to the unseen but they ignored the rest [of the Lord], to work from lack or need; so they gave away their access of the heavens, remained in the stars, and created deception. The foundation was Baal, and imagination was stolen in order to block the memory of the original seed, and to stop the growth by what they believed. The trade was even unto their children that corrupted and comingled seed of the inheritance.

We concluded that we were all attached to an ungodly tree, with far-reaching roots and tentacles (branches), which had to do with ungodly belief systems. We crafted and prayed together a prayer to deal with the false dreams and 'dream hackers', finishing just as the day ended. The next day, Jana received another word regarding dreams:

Elders are hackers. Now, <u>what has been held back and have been hacked is the same thing, which creates a belief and lack.</u> The paradigms are a veil to block goodness, and make success or failure, not just for the things in need, but for the heart that cannot see. Out of the heart flows the issues of life. This signal will attract or block the power of God, Elohim; but the dreams that have been stolen and hacked have blocked signs and wonders because of <u>lack</u>. Abundance of signs and wonders are for this generation to deliver, rescue, and perform for regeneration. The power is gathered on the <u>highway of holiness</u>. The expectations to dream will deliver or deceive and create the story, but the greatest move that is yet to come is for the prophetic discerners, the true sons. Divide the holy and profane; live in the power of His name. Learn to discern and see; then connect one to the other so the world may believe.

Notice the underlined words in Jana's prophetic word. In retrospect, this shines new light on the concept of fear being the basis of perceived lack, and how that blocks our access to the ancient path, which is God's highway of holiness. A year later, we wrote extensively about this in *Exploring Heavenly Places, Volume 12: The Mystery of the Ancient Paths*, though we did not fully realize then the magnitude to which fear is also a huge component of the enemy's right to produce false dreams.

Within days of the conclusion of the academy, I received a call from Paul regarding another false dream; he said, "I guess we haven't taken care of the dream thing." I agreed, telling him about a dream I'd had the day before, which he immediately sensed was also false. Ultimately, we agreed that what we'd accomplished at the academy had been good; but it sort of fell flat, as if we weren't quite there yet. Little did we know that more than three years would pass before we finally got enough answers to write this article and publish a new dream prayer. One thing we'd definitely learned by this point though, was the importance of always asking the Lord if a particular dream is righteous or false. But first, aside from what we learned during the academy, what else might give the enemy the right to harass us in dreams? The list is probably endless; but, as always, the Bible is a great place to start, so consider how the following might affect dreams:

> *You shall stand outside, and the man to whom you make the loan shall bring the pledge out to you. And if he is a poor man, <u>you shall not sleep in his pledge. You shall restore to him the pledge as the sun sets, that he may sleep in his cloak and bless you.</u> And it shall be righteousness for you before the* LORD *your God.*[6]

> *For <u>the thing that I fear</u> comes upon me, and <u>what I dread</u> befalls me. am not at ease, nor am I quiet; I have no rest, but trouble comes."* [7]

> *Unless the Lord builds the house, those who build it labor in vain. Unless the Lord watches over the city, the*

watchman stays awake in vain. It is in vain that you rise up early and go late to rest, <u>eating the bread of anxious toil</u>; for he gives to his beloved sleep.[8]

(Not recognizing God's truth) In peace I will both lie down and <u>sleep; for you alone, O Lord, make me dwell in safety.</u>[9]

My son, <u>do not lose sight of these — keep sound wisdom and discretion,</u> and they will be life for your soul and adornment for your neck. Then you will walk on your way securely, and your foot will not stumble. <u>If you lie down, you will not be afraid; when you lie down, your sleep will be sweet</u>.[10]

When goods increase, they increase who eat them, and what advantage has their owner but to see them with his eyes? Sweet is the sleep of a laborer, whether he eats little or much, but <u>the full stomach of the rich will not let him sleep</u>.[11]

We've previously recognized that seemingly bad dreams may not necessarily be false, but are meant to give us insight into generational sin issues; once dealt with, a person's dreams generally change. We also know that dreams happen in the heavenly realms, and it seems that either righteous or unrighteous beings may write scripts for them. Biblically however, a major root for false dreams is idolatry:

For the household gods utter nonsense, and the diviners see lies; they tell false dreams and give empty consolation.

> *Therefore the people wander like sheep; they are afflicted for lack of a shepherd.*[12]

Understanding the concept of righteous and unrighteous doors,[13] it makes sense to consider whether or not we have unwittingly allowed evil entities to gain further access to our dreams by accepting a false dream as truth. Since not believing lying prophets is a direct admonition from God, it would seem that believing our own false dreams is also an unrighteous act, which by default would give the enemy access to our dreams:

> *For thus says the LORD of hosts, the God of Israel: Do not let your prophets and your diviners who are among you deceive you, and do not listen to the dreams that they dream, for it is a lie that they are prophesying to you in my name; I did not send them, declares the LORD.*[14]

Or, do we blame our false dreams on God like Job did?

> *When I lie down I say, 'When shall I arise?' But the night is long, and I am full of tossing till the dawn… When I say, 'My bed will comfort me, my couch will ease my complaint,' then you scare me with dreams and terrify me with visions, so that I would choose strangling and death rather than my bones.*[15]

When it comes to dreams, there's a big difference between condemnation and conviction. Yes, God may send difficult dreams, but they are for His righteous purposes, perhaps to identify the generational sin issues that He wants to deal with, to prompt us to pray for someone, or perhaps to provide a prophetic 'heads-up' of something that is coming; but our first response should never be either fear or guilt. That flies in the face of scriptures:

> *God gave us a spirit not of fear but of power and love and self-control.*[16]

> *Is anyone among you suffering? Let him pray. Is anyone cheerful? Let him sing praise. Is anyone among you sick? Let him call for the elders of the church, and let them pray over him, anointing him with oil in the name of the Lord. And the prayer of faith will save the one who is sick, and the Lord will raise him up. And if he has committed sins, he will be forgiven.*[17]

> *There is therefore now no condemnation for those who are in Christ Jesus.*[18]

> *For the Lord GOD does nothing without revealing his secret to his servants the prophets.*[19]

It appears that the dream hackers may actually be enemy spies or undercover operatives who introduce fears and feed false information into our being. To make things even more difficult, the enemy also appears able to hack into righteous dreams, inserting a word or phrase here and there, which corrupt the interpretation and introduce confusion.

But, what if the Lord also hacks into false dreams? Consider a couple of my own, which happened two nights in a row. The first was on October 17, 2021; it was a long, complex dream in which Paul had invited me to go with him and some others to a shooting range. I didn't think to follow my own advice and ask the Lord if it was false, so I jumped right into the interpretation, which initially was very negative. But when I reached the end, I had a strong sense that I should consider that the righteous message might appear starting at the end and going back to the beginning. I then thought about how Hebrew is written backwards, at least from an Western point of view; and how the last chapter of Revelation reaches right back to the beginning, even before creation in Genesis 1:1:

> *Behold, I am coming soon, bringing my recompense with me, to repay each one for what he has done. I am the Alpha and the Omega, the first and the last, the beginning and the end.*[20]

Sure enough, when I read what I'd written from the bottom up, it was all about preparing the way for the return of the Lord:

- It will only be accomplished through His Spirit
- The advent of the antichrist is rapidly approaching
- Enemy attempts to take us out, which will be quickly overturned by God
- There was sure and certain knowledge that He is always here to help, and will provide the revelatory information we need

- We can neither plan ahead nor try to do things the same way we've always done while expecting the same result; it just won't happen.

Later that day, I started to tell the dream to Paul and he immediately chimed in that it felt false. He was right, but only when it was considered from start to finish. The Holy Spirit is the One who provided the reverse interpretation, without which it would have become just another false dream that was quickly discarded and forgotten.

The next day, there was another long dream that was chock-full of chaos and stress—clearly not of God. But all-the-while, I could somehow see my car driving itself straight down a busy road, never swerving to the right or left. In the dream I wondered how that could be, and was concerned that I somehow get to my car before it was in an accident or some police officer saw the driverless car, and I ended up being prosecuted for letting it happen. But then I awoke, and quickly realized the truth was that regardless of what the enemy is throwing my way, God is the One in complete control of my life (the car); He was taking me in a new direction along His ancient path, with no detours. God's spin on my two false dreams seem to highlight the truth:

And we know that <u>for those who love God all things work together for good</u>, for those who are called according to his purpose.[21]

Yes! Even false dreams can be used for good when we love him, so I would suggest that when we know a dream is false, we might do well to ask Him what to do with it.

Lots of questions still remained in 2019, but there was little breakthrough. At this point our best and, in fact, our only strategy was to ask the Lord with each dream if it was righteous or unrighteous, and to continue waiting for Him to download more revelation. Our comfort rested in the fact that as vast as the enemy's reach/influence over dreams is, God's is so much greater! Being tuned into Him is like our early warning system for an attack. Scriptures, righteous life lessons and, above all, the voice of the Holy Spirit make all the difference when we are afflicted with false dreams. The Spirit is out ultimate Teacher, and there's no better dream interpreter than Him; we have Jesus' word on that:

> *But the Helper, the Holy Spirit, whom the Father will send in my name, he will teach you all things and bring to your remembrance all that I have said to you. Peace I leave with you; my peace I give to you. Not as the world gives do I give to you. Let not your hearts be troubled, neither let them be afraid.*[22]

Fast forward to a Kingdom Institute course that was held at Aslan's Place May 10, 2022. During an introductory session regarding dreams, the discussion turned to the generational deliverance aspects of dreams. The idea that the gift of dreams and their interpretation might also be hereditary was discussed, with Abraham and his descendants being referenced to illustrate that possibility. We know for sure of that Abraham, Isaac, Jacob and Joseph were dreamers. In fact, Joseph may have inherited his dream gift from both sides since his mother's dad, Laban, also dreamed. Later on, there were a multitude of Israelite dreamers, not the least of whom were Daniel, David, and Jesus' stepfather, Joseph. So, what if we have inherited not only gifts related to dreaming, but also the iniquity that comes along with all of our ancestors abuse and misuse of dreams? What if those sins have given the enemy a right to hack our righteous dreams and or to produce false ones?

Along with the ongoing teaching there was some lively discussion and even more questions were raised:

- What happens if we have asked the Lord to remove our dreams because we were fearful of them? Repent and ask the Lord to restore them.

- What about the problem of blockages to interpreting dreams? Perhaps it's because of mixing man's wisdom with God's, either personally or generationally.

- Do scattered soul or spirit parts have the ability to dream, and would this help explain the enemy's right to hack our dreams? We believe this may be the bottom line to the hacking rights of the enemy.

Finally, after over three years, we finally had what seemed to be some important missing pieces; so we again prayed together a new prayer for further healing in our dreams. Now, we have integrated the original *Prayer to Release*

Mysteries in the Night

Dreams, the prayer we crafted at the academy in 2019, and the most recent one in 2022, to form one new Prayer.

Prayer to Release Dreams

Father, in the name of Jesus I submit this prayer on behalf of myself and my entire generational line back to before the beginning of time; as I renounce and repent for all of us who ever discounted or ignored our God-given dreams in any way.

I repent for:

- All who have believed or said, "I never dream," "God doesn't speak through dreams," or, "Dreams and dream interpretation stopped with the early church"

- Those among us who have discouraged, mocked and/or shut down dreams in any way, including asking the Lord to stop our dreams because we were fearful

- All rejection of godly dreams, thus refusing what You were trying to show us

- Any time we nurtured fear toward dreams or their interpretation

- Any time that we placed a priority on the so-called wisdom of man and ignored God's true wisdom in regard to dreams and the godly interpretation of those dreams

A Fresh Perspective on Dreams

- The worship of Baal or Moloch, which contaminated our dreams

- Using dreams for astral-projection into the heavens, false realities and ungodly worlds, in order to access and bring back that which is not allowed by You

- Using drugs of any kind to produce or enhance dreams

- Engaging in cosmic sex with fallen sons of God

- Receiving or believing false dreams and/or dream interpretations, and becoming false prophets or teachers based on ungodly dreams

- Seeking knowledge from ungodly systems instead of from the living God, especially all that trace back to Nimrod who went into the heavens to gain information

- Intentionally going to sleep in an to attempt to gain esoteric knowledge, rather than entering into the Rest of the Lord

Lord, I declare that I will no longer allow the enemy, including all ungodly rulers, thrones and other entities to interfere in my dreams. I also declare that my subconscious is open only to the true and living God, Elohim.

In Jesus' name, I now revoke any permissions given by my ancestors or myself to dream hackers or any other ungodly influence on my dreams; I totally surrender my dream life over to God.

Lord, I ask that You would retrieve all of my scattered soul and spirit parts that the enemy can no longer hold captive because of this repentance; please return them to me through the blood of Jesus and place them into my being according to Your perfect original creative design.

Lord, please disconnect me from all ungodly trees, destroying their roots and branches; please graft me into the true Branch, which is Jesus, and remove me from all ungodly belief systems.

Lord Jesus, please now close any ungodly gates, especially dream gates. Regarding my mind, my sleep and my dreams, please close all of the unrighteous doors that have been opened and open the doors of righteousness. I invite You to possess the gates of my dreams, come into them, live in them, and speak Your truths to my heart and mind.

Holy Spirit, please increase my discernment, grant me Your wisdom, knowledge and understanding regarding dreams; please counsel and teach me to understand and interpret dreams from Your perspective alone. I claim Jesus' promise:

> But the Helper, the Holy Spirit, whom the Father will send in My name, He will teach you all things, and bring to your remembrance all that I said to you.[23]

A Fresh Perspective on Dreams

Lord, please fulfill that promise in my life in regard to dreams, visions and twilight experience

---

[1] Our dear friend, Jana Green, is now at home with Jesus in Heaven. A gifted prophet, prayer minister and artist, she is greatly missed.

[2] Job 38:32

[3] Job 33:15-20

[4] Jeremiah 23:28

[5] Zechariah 10:2

[6] Deuteronomy 24:11-12

[7] Job 3:25-26

[8] Psalm 27:1-2

[9] Psalm 4:8

[10] Proverbs 21:21-23

[11] Ecclesiastes 5:11

[12] Zechariah 10:2

[13] For more information, see *Exploring Heavenly Places, Volume 3: Gates, Doors and the Grid*

[14] Jeremiah 29:8-9

[15] Job 7:4, 13-15

[16] 2 Timothy 1:7

[17] James 5:13-15

[18] Romans 8:1

[19] Amos 3:7

[20] Revelation 22:12-13

[21] Romans 8:28

[22] John 14:26-27

[23] John 14:26

Mysteries in the Night

A Fresh Perspective on Dreams

CHAPTER EIGHT:
TEACH YOUR CHILDREN WELL

As children, our dreams may have been shut inadvertently by parents or other caregivers. Perhaps, in the midst of a night terror they responded, yet again, to a child's anguished cries of fear. Longing for was a good night's sleep for a change; exhausted, yet still trying to comfort, they may have offered such unwise advice as:

- It's only a dream; forget about it and go back to sleep
- Dreams are just like make-believe or fairy tales; they don't mean anything
- You're imagining things; none of this is real
- Just ignore it; there's no such thing as monsters

That last one makes me cringe because, contrary to popular entertainment, evil spiritual beings often masquerade as monsters in children's dreams. I remember watching Disney's *Monster's Inc.* on DVD in 2003, a couple years after it was first released. I enjoyed it; even though I had recently begun moving out of my old, fundamental, religious box, and knew that the 'monsters' in the closet or under the bed could indeed be real. Many years later, during a visit to California Adventures, I went on the Monster's Inc. ride with my grandchildren. Like the movie, it was entertaining, but I was alarmed at the cute-but-subtle lies being propagated in the name of safe family fun. Friendly monsters (no such thing!) were working to rescue a child from Monstropolis, and dozens and dozens of doors floated all around us as our 'taxi' proceeded through the town. By this time, I'd come to understand both the reality and significance of dimensional doors, which can be either good or bad; or, put in a way that's a bit more sobering, righteous or unrighteous; godly or evil. An excerpt from *Exploring Heavenly Places, Volume 3: Gates, Doors, and the Grid:*[1]

> We often visit heavenly places in our dreams; places where God may reveal His truths through visual symbols, and doors are a good example of how everyday objects may hold a variety of meanings in 'dreamspeak'. We've already seen how Jesus relates to a door, so He may be the One to whom a dream about a door points; but the meaning may also relate to our common understanding, with a door representing any of the aspects of its definition (i.e. opportunity, entry, access). Going a bit farther, a description of the door(s) may offer enhanced understanding. For example, we would probably think of a squeaky door as one that needs to be oiled, but in a dream it could indicate a need of the Anointing; a back door may indicate something that is secret or in the past, and a front door the future; going from one door to another could indicate witnessing; and more than one closed door might represent either a choice that needs to be made or some kind of blockage.

How dangerous if a child believes the lie early on that the monsters/demonic entities in their dreams should be ignored because they're not real! Such a belief sets the stage for a lifetime of skepticism, both about the importance of dreams and the reality of the spiritual threats that may be revealed in them. How many adults have failed to receive generational prayer and healing regarding issues that the Lord revealed in dreams because they believed well-meaning-but-misconstrued advice of parents or caregivers? Only God knows.

To be honest though, when my own child was small; I don't even remember how I reacted to his dreams, or if we even talked much about them, but that was then and this is now. Fast forward through a lot of years, and there have been occasions while babysitting for my grandchildren when one of them would awaken with a night terror. In those instances, they were so upset that any 'teaching moment' was impossible. All I could do was hold and comfort them because they were so afraid; softly speaking or singing, all-the-while praying silently for the Lord to intervene on their behalf. In some cases, especially with very young children, that may be the best approach.

Clearly, the response in such situations must be age appropriate, so I checked in with a few moms of young children to glean from their wisdom. Interestingly, teaching their kids about Jesus' love and His 'super-powers' over the bad guys or monsters was a common theme. Then, as the kids matured enough to understand the Gospel and accepted Him as Savior, their identity in Christ became an important focus; and teaching about taking authority in His name over the evil in dreams became possible. One mom taught her daughter how she could rebuke the enemy and send him packing; and the little girl immediately began doing just that. She now takes care of business and then tells her mom the next morning what has happened; serious stuff, but beyond cute when related by a second grader!

Regardless of age, a parent would be wise to consider generational prayers on behalf of themselves and their children in order to reveal and remove any rights the enemy has to afflict them with night terrors, as well as to deal with generational issues that have been revealed.

One mother of a little girl (subsequently referred to as K) first began emailing me about K's dreams when she was only four. Below are a few of our interchanges:

May, 2018:

> K dreams. I've been asking her more lately about what she dreams. I'm not sure what to think about some of them. She's four, and while her vocabulary is large for her age it's still limited. I've written them all down, but haven't really come to understand what they mean. I'm still learning to understand my own dreams, and I could use some help. Her most recent dream in the way she told me; the (parenthesized) parts are what I added:

There was a nice lady making a cake. She had purple hair (she pointed to the crayon she was coloring with; it was a purple, maroon color). She had a big chef's hat and apron; they were both white. The cake was white and pink and sparkly, with cherries and yellow shiny pennies (gold coins?). She said the lady had hands like mine (I'm not totally sure I know what that means). She said that the lady was making the cake for everyone.

My response:
Wow! I don't think I've done any dream interpretations for such a small child, so this is exciting. I think the main thing to remember about understanding your daughter's dreams is to see them through her eyes, and perhaps talk/pray through them with her. Little kids are amazingly open to discernment and seeing/hearing what God is saying. You can suggest that she ask Jesus what specific aspects of a dream mean. One technique that might be very effective is to encourage your daughter to remember what the dream looked like and then encourage her to invite Jesus to show her where He is in the dream; then have her ask Him what He wants her to know about it. You may be amazed at what happens!

For this particular dream, it's all good, and again, it may depend on your daughter's perspective; but I'll try to address it as if it were one of my five-year-old granddaughters.

For a little girl, a beautiful cake probably means a very happy, joyous time such as a birthday party, so it could have an element of the joy of the Lord in it - perhaps joyful expectation or promise. From a standard dream dictionary perspective, cake and money can be about provision, and a chef can represent Jesus; though in this case I suspect she more likely represents the Holy Spirit, who frequently is presented as feminine in dreams; it could also be an angel. Purple hair could just be fun from a child's perspective, or could have to do with royalty from a dream dictionary perspective. White is about righteousness and gold is about God's glory. I think the hands look like yours because as her mom you represent God's love, and in this dream He is basically showing her His love/joy/provision, and also that it's available for all who will receive it.

August, 2018:

K woke up this morning crying. She said she had a bad dream. Someone 'lit up' her sister and me. She said we weren't hurt but we were on fire. I wasn't sure what to think. It's hard to piece together what she tells me; it's not always in order. There was a grocery store, a horse, and a boy with a blue and brown hat. Most of what she said was jumbled up. That is proving to be the biggest challenge, actually understanding what she is telling me and getting her to say it in order.

Anyway, after talking together we prayed. I asked God to show her where He was in her dream. We sat a minute, and I asked her what God said. She said He was beating up the bad guys. Then she mentioned that she ate an apple out of the basket and was healed, and her sister was ok too. She hadn't mentioned any of this earlier; she was just upset. She calmed down after we prayed. I asked if her dream changed after I prayed. She said she didn't know. It would be pretty wonderful if it changed after we prayed; yes, pretty wonderful.

My friend also related a couple of instances in which her children's dreams and night-time experiences were apparently influenced by physical objects in the home:

April, 2019:

During our recent move, the Lord started speaking to me about teaching children to 'hear' him. He showed me examples in the Bible of children who knew the ways of God but didn't know Him. He showed me the consequences of only teaching children how to serve him but not teaching them who He is and how He speaks. Now, He's showing me why they can't just know how He speaks but they HAVE to know who He is.

Since we have been in the new house, our dreams have changed. K woke up twice in one day with the same really bad dream, once in the morning and again that night. We prayed and she went back to sleep. Then I had a very creepy thing happen. I put a doll I have had for years on the mantle of our fireplace. After praying with K, I went back into the living room to pray/study/read and I noticed the doll didn't look right. I felt led to take a picture of it. When I looked at the picture, I noticed two faces in the right corner. I sent the picture to a friend without saying anything, and then asked her about it the next day. She saw them too. That doll and all the others went in the garbage truck the next day. K hasn't had another bad dream since. The house feels better too.

September, 2019:

K's younger sister had been given some clothes from someone I wasn't sure about, and I noticed that they both started waking up during the night shortly after getting them. The house started to feel a little funky too, like there was someone extra there that I couldn't see. I put the clothes in the trunk of the car and they slept all night that night. They were gotten rid of the next day, and the house feels better too.

In other instances, K's dreams seemed to be the result of an un-addressed fear:

Most of K's recent dreams have had to do with me and something happening that seemed bad to her but wasn't, at least not that I could tell. One was of me going to dance on the stage at church and she didn't want me to. I told her I was going to and did, and she went and cried in the bushes outside.

A Fresh Perspective on Dreams

For context, I had recently started singing Sunday mornings at church, so I explained to her that mommy was going to be obedient to God no matter what He asks me to do, and she will be ok. She hasn't had another issue with me being up there since.

Moral of the above stories: pay attention to your children's dreams, and:

Train up a child in the way he should go; even when he is old he will not depart from it.[2]

---

[1] http://aslansplace.3dcartstores.com/Exploring-Heavenly-Places-Volume-3--Gates-Doors-and-the-Grid--Paperback_p_568.html

[2] Proverbs 22:6

Mysteries in the Night

Chapter Nine:
A Heart for Every Generation

The importance of teaching our children well cannot be understated, especially regarding spiritual matters:

> *Give ear, O my people, to my teaching; incline your ears to the words of my mouth! I will open my mouth in a parable; I will utter dark sayings from of old, things that we have heard and known, that our fathers have told us. We will not hide them from their children, but tell to the coming generation the glorious deeds of the* LORD, *and his might, and the wonders that he has done. He established a testimony in Jacob and appointed a law in Israel, which he commanded our fathers to teach to their children, that the next generation might know them, the children yet unborn, and arise and tell them to their children, so that they should set their hope in God and not forget the works of God, but keep his commandments; and that they should not be like their fathers, a stubborn and rebellious generation, a generation whose heart was not steadfast, whose spirit was not faithful to God.*[1]

This is a responsibility I took very seriously while raising our son; he was my primary focus for years, and now my heart is blessed to observe how he teaches his own children about the Lord. The love my grandchildren have for Jesus is one of the greatest blessings of my life! That said, the older I get, the more my passion grows to train up new generations, not only within my own family but also among all of those that God places before me. My frequent prayer is:

> *O God, from my youth you have taught me, and I still proclaim your wondrous deeds. So even to old age and gray hairs, O God, do not forsake me, until I proclaim your might to another generation, your power to all those to come.*[2]

The Lord has been answering that prayer in surprising ways during recent years, often connecting me to younger people I've never even heard of until one day I receive a call, text or email. Suddenly, we're off on an exciting journey through their dreams; and the Lord allows me to observe as He not only brings new levels of deliverance and healing, but also downloads greater and greater levels of wisdom and understanding into their lives. Let me be very, very clear; this is all about Him, for without Him I am nothing. In fact, during some of our sessions the silent cry from my heart to Him is often, "Oh God, help! I don't have a clue what to say or do. Please, let Your strength be evident in my weakness." Fortunately, He never fails to come through for me.

Briana Lassiter first began emailing me about her dreams, as well as those of her husband and daughter, in 2018. Since then, we've had multiple opportunities to spend time together. Sometimes we're on the phone for minutes or hours, either working through complex dreams or just catching up. Other times we're texting, and still other times we've been together at conferences in various places, and our friendship has blossomed into a beyond-special blessing for both of us.

Briana is one of the moms I contacted regarding how they handle dreams with their children, and she immediately began praying about what she should say. I also interviewed her daughter, Jackie, about what she's learned from her mother about dreams, but more about that in the next chapter. Following are the words the Lord told Briana to write; they are both humbling and gratifying to me; they illustrate my heart's desire to proclaim His might and power to other generations, as well as one way in which He has answered my prayer:

> Most of what I know to teach my daughter about dreams has come from what I've learned from Barbara. It feels like God has brought things full circle through Jackie and Barb's conversations about what Jackie knows about dreams.
>
> Years ago, frustrated by the nonsense and new age approach to dreams, I asked God to show me who He wanted me to learn from about dreams. He led me to Barbara's YouTube dream teachings.
>
> Little did I know then that I would not only gain a very treasured friend in Barb but that through her books and videos, my enthusiastic sharing of truth to almost everyone I knew would lead to an entire small community learning, sharing, and gaining

new radical levels of freedom in dreams and their interpretation.

To me, it illustrates this precious principle that plays out time and time again in the Bible, "If you, then I..." It's taken directly from 2 Chronicles 7:14 and Jeremiah 33:3, although it pops up everywhere from beginning to end of the Bible. I think it illustrates the give-and-take of relationship over religion, and how action is promised from both us and God!

I like to call it the Intimacy Principle, as it is the promise that when we call, He will respond and do more than we ever imagined:

> *Call upon me and I will answer thee, exceedingly above all that we could ask or think.*[3]

To me, it is the proof for my life, that when I ask, God will always answer and it is now what I stand on to encourage others to test the Intimacy Principle for themselves and see what happens.

Intimacy – what a concept; and one that goes so much deeper than a common description of physical closeness. In its broader definition, intimacy refers to a close, familiar, affectionate or loving personal relationship. Intimacy occurs among those who trust one another enough to share things they would never talk about to most people. These are types of conversations and experiences that occur only among the closest of friends and loved ones, and God earnestly desires just such a relationship with each one of us:

> *Behold, I stand at the door and knock. If anyone hears my voice and opens the door, I will come in to him and eat with him, and he with me.*[4]

God loves to communicate intimately with us, and His desire for such an intimacy is closely tied to dreams:

> *For God speaks in one way, and in two, though man does not perceive it. In a dream, in a vision of the night, when deep sleep falls on men, while they slumber on their beds, then he opens the ears of men and terrifies them with warnings, that he may turn man aside from his deed and conceal pride from a man; he keeps back his soul from the pit, his life from perishing by the sword.*[5]

In *Dreamspeak*, I wrote:

> Dreamspeak is a term that is often used in regard to the symbolism of dreams and visions, but my favorite definition comes from Paul Cox, who responded to a text informing him that the Lord had provided the sub-title with, "Yeah, the language that only you and God know." So true! God communicates with each person in a unique and highly individualized way; and while there are a lot of commonalities, there is no one-size-fits-all method to understand exactly what He is saying every single time.

Isn't it amazing to know that Almighty God wants to communicate with us so badly that He encrypts a special dream language for each of us? Also from *Dreamspeak:*

> Pursue intimacy with God as relentlessly as you would pursue a potential love interest. Talk to Him, walk with Him, listen to Him; learn to recognize and understand His voice any time of the day or night, whether awake or asleep.

This is what I see happening, not only in Briana but also in many others as well. Ours is a critical time in history, a time in which Jesus' words are beyond relevant:

> *Then he said to his disciples, "The harvest is plentiful, but the laborers are few; therefore pray earnestly to the Lord of the harvest to send out laborers into his harvest.*[6]

With God's final harvest on our horizon, there has never been a better time to raise up our children in the way they should go and enter into His promise:

> *But the steadfast love of the* LORD *is from everlasting to everlasting on those who fear him, and his righteousness to children's children, to those who keep his covenant and remember to do his commandments.* [7]

---

[1] Psalm 78:1-8
[2] Psalm 71:17-18

[3] Jeremiah 33:3 paraphrased
[4] Revelation 3:20
[5] Job 33:14-18
[6] Matthew 9:37-38
[7] Psalm 103:17-18

Mysteries in the Night

Chapter Ten:
Through the Eyes of a Child

From Briana's first introductory email, "My six-year-old daughter's dream; or as she says, experience":

> I was in a heavenly place; it was God's place. Beautiful trees of good fruit and hats that say, "I love God." Everything was gold, and Jesus was wearing the same hat I just told you about. He was wearing a crown and a vest, and his face said, "I love you." I felt like I was with God; I felt like we were friends.

My response:

> Jackie's dream is amazing, and it's so fun because little kids' dreams are so un-filtered by what we think we know, and simply reflect God's truth. Her dream of being in a heavenly place illustrates the truth that we are seated with Christ in heavenly places; and the images of gold (glory), royalty, and friendship with Jesus are how we all need to encounter Him. Even the feeling that she was with God seems like a child's version of the truth of Jesus' teaching regarding oneness with God.

The Lord impressed me that it would be a good idea to interview Briana and Jackie together, and then to share a child's perspective on dreams for this book. To say I was

Mysteries in the Night

blown away by what happened is an understatement! Jackie, who is now ten years old, answered every question I asked with the maturity of an adult, saying, "Well, my mom told me..." or, "I learned from my mom that..." Clearly, she's a shining example of what is possible when a child is trained up in the way she should go!

At one point I asked Briana if she ever prays generational prayers over Jackie while she's sleeping. Her response was, "Well, duh!!!" I guess a simple 'yes' didn't quite cover it.

We decided to tackle one of Jackie's recent dreams that she didn't understand yet, and then work through it exactly like we would with an adult. The dream is then followed by our conversation: Jackie's dream:

> Jackie: I am in the middle of a war and I suddenly disappear and turn into black dust. I can watch myself disappear. (Mom was shocked because this is an actual scene from a movie.)
>
> Bri: It's Marvel's *Avengers: Infinity War,* and she has never seen or heard about this!
>
> Barb: Ask why am I in a war scene Lord?
>
> Jackie: I'm hearing it's a spiritual battle I am in.
>
> Barb: ATL (ask the Lord) why is there black dust. Is that important?
>
> Jackie: I'm not hearing anything.

Barb: When we're not hearing anything sometimes we aren't asking the right question; or it could mean we just need more practice using our gifts. Try asking, "Lord do we need to know more about the spiritual battle?"

Jackie: I'm hearing yes!

Barb: Ask, "What do I need to know about the battle?

Jackie: I'm hearing it's another generational dream.

Barb: So, Lord, what kind of generational issue?

Bri: I heard and saw people from the past and future in our generational line, and Jackie in the line. Some were mighty warriors who stepped into their identity, and some who had not; even though I could see who they were meant to be. I have a sense this is about who Jackie is, who God created her to be, her purpose, calling, gifts and identity.

Jackie: Lord, is there anything you want me to know about my identity? (Pause) I keep thinking about secret superheroes with a secret identity.

Barb: Ask the Lord what He wants you to know about being a superhero?

Bri: I heard, "Your identity is being hidden in Me; although the enemy wants you to disappear, you are actually being hidden in Me."

Jackie: I'm hearing the Lord saying, "You're a superhero because they are strong and courageous, and use their powers for good!"

Barb: I heard Zechariah 4:6, *Not by power or by might, but by My Spirit says the Lord.* What does that mean to you?

Jackie: I don't know!

Barb: Ask, "Lord, does this mean that if I rely on your Spirit, I can be a superhero?

Jackie and Mom immediately heard, "YES!" Meanwhile, Barbara had a sense of being knocked back in her chair while hearing, "You already are!"

Barb: So, let's get back to the dream knowing that it's about you relying on Him and His power to be a superhero. Does that mean it's about relying on His power in your identity to become a superhero? And, does it mean that in your everyday life you can be a superhero?

Jackie: I'm hearing, "Yes!"

Barbara encouraged Briana to craft a generational prayer to take care of the enemy's rights.

Bri: Lord, I repent on behalf of myself and all those in my generational line who relied on ourselves and our own power, and did not rely on You and your power. Please forgive us for trying to use our gifts to step into our identity apart from you and your Spirit. Lord, I know that as a result of this sin, we were never fully able to step into our true identity, gifts or callings; because without You we can do nothing. Please, now remove all associated curses, iniquities and consequences of this sin and restore to us fully our identity, gifts, callings and ability to totally rely on you, in Jesus' name.

Barb: Go back to the dream Jackie. Are you still black dust?

Jackie: I'm hearing Psalm 300:9, but there isn't a Psalm 300:9!

Barb: Ask the Lord if it's something that happened 309 years ago?

Jackie: It's a generational curse placed on our family 309 years ago.

Barb: Do we need to know what it is, or can you just give Jesus permission to deal with it?

Bri: I feel the curse is that we would never come into the fullness of our identity. We give you permission Jesus, to deal with this curse.

Barb: I am sensing that Psalm 1 is the blessing to replace the curse.

Bri: I knew we would end up in Psalm 1 today! Verse 4 is what happens to the wicked; they are like the chaff that the wind drives away! The enemy intended you to be blown away Jackie, but that's actually what the Lord says will happen to them!

Barb: Jackie, Ask the Lord if there's a superhero name He wants you to have.

Jackie: I heard, "It's Jackie!"

Barb: That's wonderful. Here are a few pointers you may want to think about to help you understand your dreams:

- You're very artistic, so when you are going through a dream, it may be helpful to draw a picture of your dreams before you go through it with the Lord. Then do an after picture showing how the dream changed as you prayed through it.

- You can also ask, "Jesus will you get into this dream with me and show me what you want me to see?

- Keep practicing using your gifts, your knower.

- Write the dream down and pray through it and ask questions. Usually when I do that, the pieces come together more easily.

- Ask the Lord, what He wants to teach you about your gifts and dreams?

A Fresh Perspective on Dreams

Subsequently, Briana, Jackie and I had another conversation about Jackie's dreams. This time we dealt with two shorter dreams, both of which dealt with painful rejection and one of which was a hurtful memory within a dream that was replayed exactly as it had happened. Initially, she was hesitant to talk about them, and her very-wise mom assured her that she didn't have to if she wasn't ready; so with the pressure off, Jackie decided to be brave and go for it. The courage of this ten-year-old was amazing to watch! Afterall, many adults aren't willing to be transparent enough to face such pain head on, burying it as deeply as possible so they don't have to feel the anguish of the situation.

Throughout, the Lord was kind and gentle, giving Jackie understanding about such situations in general, while also comforting her about the two that have affected her. He even threw in a surprise or two along the way. At one point Jackie suddenly had a brilliant smile on her face after she asked Jesus what seemed like a simple yes-or-no question. and exclaimed, "I've never heard Him say that before!" We asked what He said and she replied, "Sure." Her delight was in the fact that Jesus surprised her by saying something (sure) in a way she never expected.

Along the way, but Briana and I had opportunities to inject a little teaching, mostly giving biblical insights into what was happening. When all was said and done, all sadness and tears were completed wiped away and a very happy-and-content little girl headed off to grab a snack and go outside for a while.

Mysteries in the Night

Briana and Jackie should not be the exception to the rule in Christian households. Kids are much smarter that we often give them credit for, and are capable of learning to deal with the dreams that the Lord gives them. All it takes are parents, grandparents and Christian friends who are willing to equip them, just like they would any other young believer. Heed the biblical precedent:

> *"Only take care, and keep your soul diligently, lest you forget the things that your eyes have seen, and lest they depart from your heart all the days of your life. Make them known to your children and your children's children — how on the day that you stood before the LORD your God at Horeb, the LORD said to me, 'Gather the people to me, that I may let them hear my words, so that they may learn to fear me all the days that they live on the earth, and that they may teach their children so.'"* [1]
>
> *Then children were brought to him that he might lay his hands on them and pray. The disciples rebuked the people, but Jesus said, "Let the little children come to me and do not hinder them, for to such belongs the kingdom of heaven."* [2]

---

[1] Deuteronomy 4:9-10
[2] Matthew 19:13-14

CHAPTER ELEVEN:
FANTASTICAL FAITH

Why fantastical? Mainly because that's the name the Lord gave me for this chapter; but I imagine it's also because 'fantastic' just doesn't seem to do justice to the kind of faith that is required to enter into the mysteries of the night. 'Fantastical' refers to something that's so strange and wonderful that it could be something out of a story of fantasy or science fiction. It can also be about something so unusual or extreme that one wonders how it could even be true, which is why dreams are often treated as meaningless nonsense.

Our God is beyond understanding so, by definition, He is fantastical. Therefore, such a faith is often required to delve into the truths He shares in our dreams:

> *For my thoughts are not your thoughts, neither are your ways my ways, declares the LORD. For as the heavens are higher than the earth, so are my ways higher than your ways and my thoughts than your thoughts.*[1]

> *Now faith is the assurance of things hoped for, the conviction of things not seen...And without faith it is impossible to please him, for whoever would draw near to God must believe that he exists and that he rewards those who seek him.*[2]

On November 8, 2022, Bri documented two prophetic words:

> Spirit of Truth: "The spirit of the living God is upon you, Briana Lassiter; and indeed in you, mighty and roaring. As I am United in Me, One, without religiosity. Puzzles, puzzles, and there are keys; keys for all your needs (seeing me with a black, liquid-looking coat with keys inside). Secrecy, secrecy is the key to this mission; for in My submission you will find the secrets, the keys, the answers to eternity (seeing the moment the Lord's heart became one with mine, and it looked like an infusion of flowing power in a figure 8, the heart becoming one was a key)."

> Spirit of knowledge: "Listen my daughter, for I have much to say. Do not ignore your dreams in the night, for in them I am speaking to thee. Do not cower, shrink back and be afraid. Press in for I AM. The Ancient of Days has much to say to thee and knowledge, My knowledge, will guide the way. Press in for the Daniel anointing and you will receive."

The next morning, November 9th, she had a dream that was clearly from the Lord, and it had to do with current personal issues in her life as well as her whole family. We worked through it, but she didn't have her final 'ah-ha' that it was finished.

The next day, November 10th, Briana awoke in the morning feeling as if she was being stabbed, and we dealt with that by re-visiting the unresolved dream from the previous day. The conclusion, which was the ah-ha, was that there were parasitic systems of relationships and ungodly connections. The Lord did a deeper deliverance for both her and her family, removing these previously unknown, unrighteous spiritual connections to the fallen sons.[3] Bri understood then that the stabbing feelings were discernment of stabs of jealousy or envy from the fallen sons. Then she heard:

> The enemy cannot re-establish these connections so there is mass panic and chaos, which is good because you are in My peace, and I am already crushing the chaos with My teeth of peace.

> The stabbings you are feeling, Bri, are not just about thee; it's the enemy's last-ditch attempt to abort what I am doing. But look closely at the stabbing. What do you see? It's a false reality. The enemy cannot function in My truth so they are functioning in this false reality.

> Great! You have all been removed from this system of false reality. This happened when I removed and cleansed your connections; for I AM is setting the lonely and the orphans into families that **I DESIGNED**; not the enemy.

Our conversation continued as we explored more of what God seemed to be doing:

Barb: Does this have to do with Jesus' words that the elect will be deceived if possible?

Bri: I'm remembering the word received last week about how if we didn't submit to this deeper layer of deliverance, the enemy would twist things; twisting our hearts away, and we would be surprised at who fell away.

Barb : Is it possible that many people who we think are following the Spirit are actually following the false Holy Spirit? They think they're following the Lord but are falling into the trap of false belief systems. It's kind of like a small child playing house with a toy kitchen and fake food; it feels real to them but it's not. What if there are many who have already been deceived? It's not about salvation per se; it's deception about the power and the grace and the moving of the Holy Spirit. A lot of people think they are full to overflowing with the Spirit, but they don't really have an intimate relationship with the Spirit. Their false reality is a misconception of who the Holy Spirit is and what the Spirit's doing. There may be something about the intangibility of the Spirit that people have a hard time with, so they latch onto any spiritual manifestation; but without discernment, incorrect conclusions are drawn. Is this a clash of the house of Wisdom against the house of Folly? [4]

Bri: We are God's house **if** we hold fast our confidence and hope in Him till the end:

> *(For every house is built by someone, but the builder of all things is God.) ... but Christ is faithful over God's house as a son. And we are his house, if indeed we hold fast our confidence and our boasting in our hope.*[5]

What if we are corrupting the house He built for us by living in the false house with false ideologies?

> *By faith we understand that the universe was created by the word of God, so that what is seen was not made out of things that are visible.*[6]

Is the entire false system built on the whole skeptical mindset that needs proof, tangible proof, in order to believe? That's a false reality; there are many false realities.

Is this the enemy's end-time attempt to recreate the Tower-of-Babel experience where the people were in unholy unity?

Barb: It seems to be about either the inability to perceive God, or false perceptions of Him:

> *Behold, he passes by me, and I see him not; he moves on, but I do not perceive him.*[7]

Bri: Then it becomes a false reality when we get caught up in our pain; we get wrapped up in that and focus on a false reality instead of the reality that God is here right now, all the time. We have access to His kingdom but we get caught up in all the illusions that He's not here, so we don't see Him, we don't believe Him. Our faith is in the wrong thing:

> *Indeed, in their case the prophecy of Isaiah is fulfilled that says: "You will indeed hear but never understand, and you will indeed see but never perceive." For this people's heart has grown dull, and with their ears they can barely hear, and their eyes they have closed, lest they should see with their eyes and hear with their ears and understand with their heart and turn, and I would heal them.' But blessed are your eyes, for they see, and your ears, for they hear.[8]*

It didn't seem like the Lord was finished with us, but we weren't sure where to go next, so I suggested that Briana ask Him to remind her of another dream that He'd like to talk about. She did, and it was a fantastical doozy from January 2022, which we determined after an attempt at that time to interpret it, that this dream is so prophetic we wouldn't understand it until it happened. Now, it dovetails both with actual current events in Bri's family as well as the world:

> I am with a small group of friends. Daniel S is with me, and the Lord said he represents characteristics of Daniel and David. We are on a large sandy hill and at the bottom, is the Pacific Ocean.

A Fresh Perspective on Dreams

> I get washed out into the water and am scared. There's a massive group of jellyfish in the water that are stinging me and I am angry, and shout, "This is why I hate the ocean!" Others with me casually laugh and say this is just how it is in the ocean; you get used to it. I can feel the stings, and I am headed towards a massive wave. The group shouts instructions at me on about how to avoid a large number of jellyfish coming towards me.
>
> Somehow, I am caught up in a monster wave, maybe six feet. The group shouts instructions on how to surf the wave, which I do without a surfboard. There are many surfers who have come to surf this specific wave and are angry that not only did I surf it, I did it as someone who was just washed out in the ocean and didn't even know how to surf.

Insights thus far:
Bri sensed was that the six-foot waves represent the coming six years; and the surfers represent religious people.

Barbara sensed that six years for those of us who are determined to follow the Spirit will be like the dream; we will surf the waves of the Spirit without a surfboard where there's nothing man made; it's just you and the Lord.

The dream continues:

> I am somehow washed out to sea, and am now a few miles from the sandy hill island; only Daniel S

is with me. I see a few beings trying to trespass the boundary of the ocean and think to myself that they will find themselves in trouble; but I swim on, thinking to get back to the sandy hill island. A man with a large, inflatable lifeboat that looks like an air mattress calls out to me and offers a lift. I accept and we swim to it, only to discover the man is not maneuvering the raft correctly. I take charge and show him how to move with the waves so we all don't all drown.

We cross a massive orange cord, spanning from one side of the ocean to the other. I know it is a boundary line and I think to myself as I cross, "This is a ley line." Many on the life raft, jump out and disappear into the ocean now, and I thought, "How strange and foolish."

Further insights:

- The many who jump out of the boat represent those who are deceived and fall away from the gospel
- As we ask about the boundary line, Bri sees a picture of sheep and goats being separated, and Barbara heard 'line of demarcation', which means significant separation
- This ley line is something that it seems the enemy cannot cross
- Sandy hill island represents something in the spirit appearing in the physical, and Bri hears the Lord say, "It's a portal, a spiritual phenomenon)

A Fresh Perspective on Dreams

Back to the dream:

> Once I reach the sandy hill island, I head toward an enchanted island. A witch there has captured many of our own, but I am coming for Justin (Bri's husband), who is being held prisoner in a cell. He and his small group have not been enchanted although everyone else has been. I know that being deceived by religion is an aspect of the enchantment.
>
> The whole place is a facade of goodness, as if you covered poop in glitter and called it good. Glitter and bright colors are everywhere, as well as the scent of a cheap perfume. The captives have been charmed into only being positive, saying only what the witch wants to hear. Many are our people, but many others are righteous beings who have been captured and enchanted as well. They are all afraid and try to stop me, but I go to Justin's cell and tell him I'm coming to break him out. I know I can count on him and the small group with him to help battle our way out once they're out of the cell; but I don't know how we'll do it yet. As I contemplate, I am discovered by the witch because the fear of the other enchanted inhabitants has alerted her.
>
> I have brought my four wedding rings to trade for Justin's life. I think to myself that four is a door.

More insights:

Bri: When I woke, the Lord said it is important where these four rings came from. In real life we bought the first two in two different towns, River Gate and White House, when we got engaged. The other two were bought for our ten-year anniversary; they were from the diamond district in Israel, where the ancient settlement of Noah's son, Japheth, is said to be. River Gate has to do with the river of life; and Jesus is given to us like an engagement ring, and they represent covenant relationships. I'm hearing, "White House has to do with ruling and reigning, and pursuing the covenant promise of Japheth "

> *May God enlarge Japheth, and let him dwell in the tents of Shem, and let Canaan be his servant.*[9]

Barb thought of Isaiah's words:

> *Enlarge the place of your tent, and let the curtains of your habitations be stretched out; do not hold back; lengthen your cords and strengthen your stakes. For you will spread abroad to the right and to the left, and your offspring will possess the nations and will people the desolate cities.*[10]

Barb asked, "What does this have to do with the wedding rings?"

Bri heard, "It is the covenant relationship. As you abide in Me, I will lead you into the place which you shall be."

The dream continues:

A Fresh Perspective on Dreams

The witch does not agree to the exchange, but that's okay because as soon as she gets ahold of the rings she is under their power and does not like that. She tries to enchant me but I say, "Yod Hey Vav Hey"; which means, "The name of the Lord is my strong and mighty tower." I am in it, and safe, and she cannot enchant me; so she is very distressed and leaves, I assume, to gather reinforcements.

I try to break the enchantment on the others but they are too afraid. The witch has tricked them into believing even their throw up is great (reminds me of the movie, *Trolls*), but I puke on one of the witch's statues and show everyone; saying, "See, back in the real world, this is how disgusting it looks." Something happened when I did that; I felt the witch's anger, and she came back. But above the statue was a hidden map on the wall; it was a map with directions and battle plans. As I tore it off the wall, I spoke in tongues, loudly and mockingly, to the witch. I knew the interpretation was something like, "She thought we would never find you, she thought we would never win, she thought we were weak and stupid under her spell, she thought we would never find you."

The witch became very afraid, and my possession of this map broke the prison cell. Justin's little group came out fighting and we ran out of the castle. We turned back and saw that the witch was sending a massive wave to swallow us. Also, the whole group of enchanted godly beings, along with the enchanted captives who were *bene elohim* (sons of God), were being sent to kill us.

I'd had enough so I called for Jesus, the Lion of Judah, to come and help us. As I did, He appeared with a roar that broke the spell on the beings. Now, I had a sword in my hand so I turned and, with all my might, struck the waves shouting, "Yod Hey Vav Hey." The waves shattered like broken glass and disappeared. It was shocking because the water had looked and felt so real.

I now had Justin and, somehow, the four rings back. Plus, all the captives were freed, and the witch's whole world destroyed. I was overjoyed!

Barb: I heard, "You shall know the truth, and the truth shall set you free." [11]

Bri: Does this have to do with my role in the harvest? Is the witch's castle a stronghold of fear? Fear is what enables the enemy's power.

Barb: Hmmm, interesting that the witch could smell the fear of her captives. Perhaps the enemy also smells our fear, escalates it and incapacitates us, causing us to become ineffective warriors in the Lord's battle.

Our exploration on that day concluded, but did you notice the fantastical way the Lord put it all together, as only He could? A modern screenwriter couldn't have come up with so many twists and turns! This dream includes just about everything but the kitchen sink; starting with being washed out to sea and encountering stinging jellyfish and massive waves, only to then surf one of them with neither knowledge nor surfboard. It continues with spiritual beings trying to bypass god-ordained boundaries, an out-of-nowhere rescue (by a rescuer who seemingly doesn't know what he's doing!), deception, imprisonment, wedding rings and covenant promises, an enchanted island complete with a witch and her evil spells, fear, escape, a Hebraic declaration and total victory through Christ Jesus. Then on top of all of that, the whole thing relates both to current and prophetic events.

Talking to Bri a few days later, she told me that the Lord had been showing her there's still more to understand that hasn't been unpacked yet, and she'd shared her dream with another friend. Sure enough, there were more insights; a few of which are shared here:

- I wonder if the surfers are a type of religious people who try to tell you how to surf in the Spirit but who have no aim or goal or vision beyond the surfing (those who say you can only have one primary gifting, for example). They cannot fathom how you're surfing without the construct they've been given (education, spiritual constructs, etc.). They get mad/jealous when you do it anyway!

- The people in the water shouting instructions on how to avoid the jellyfish could be those who are in the

Spirit, but are still stuck in the mindset of religion. They think they are surfing the waves of the Spirit, but are still stuck in small-minded ways of thinking about God and how He does things; like those who believe you can only have one evangelistic gift instead of expressing every aspect of God, and then getting upset when you surf past those beliefs.

- As you took the map from the wall, the cell opened for Justin. I submit that as you go and do the things the Lord has for you, that act will set your and others free. What is an action item that takes steps towards God's plan? For me, it's to renew my passport by the end of the month. For you, I get, "Packing up"? (He didn't know at the time that the Lord had already been speaking to Bri about packing up her house as they prepare for a long-distance move.)

Reviewing this chapter with Briana, she responded anew to the jealousy of the fallen sons of God as illuminated above, as well as to that just mentioned by our friend. She spoke of her anger that in today's Church we are so often taught that we just have to endure difficulties that come our way as well as jealousy over our giftings and abilities. She added, "I am not content to just follow someone's instruction to just endure attacks and avoid conflicts; I want them gone!" Her anger is reminiscent of Jesus' righteous indignation:

The Passover of the Jews was at hand, and Jesus went up to Jerusalem. In the temple he found those who were selling oxen and sheep and pigeons, and the money-

changers sitting there. And making a whip of cords, he drove them all out of the temple, with the sheep and oxen. And he poured out the coins of the money-changers and overturned their tables. And he told those who sold the pigeons, "Take these things away; do not make my Father's house a house of trade." His disciples remembered that it was written, "Zeal for your house will consume me." [12]

It is interesting to note is that the original witch/enchanted island dream happened almost a year ago, and at the time Bri felt like it prophetically represented 6 years. As of this writing it's already been eleven months, so it would seem to be a pretty safe assumption that much more will be revealing throughout the next five years.

Do you see how complex dreams can be? There are so many things to consider, far beyond one simple interpretation that gets filed away and often forgotten. The journey through just this one chapter has involved multiple people working on interpretations, current personal implications within Bri's life and family, messages about the current state of affairs within the Body of Christ, prophetic implications that have yet to be realized, scriptural parallels, deliverance, discernment, instruction and encouragement; and yet we've apparently only scratched the surface of all that God wants to reveal as time goes by

Fantastical faith in our fantastical God is required, to say the least!

---

[1] Isaiah 55:8-9
[2] Hebrews 1:1,6
[3] Genesis 6:1-5, Job 1:6-7, 2:1-2
[4] See Proverbs 9
[5] Hebrews 3:4,6
[6] Hebrews 11:3
[7] Job 9:11
[8] Matthew 13:14-16
[9] Genesis 9:27
[10] Isaiah 54:2-3
[11] John 8:32
[12] John 2:13-17

A Fresh Perspective on Dreams

CHAPTER TWELVE:
GOD'S SOCIAL NETWORKING

Y2K, the year 2000 and the turn of the century, is ancient history for many millennials today; some hadn't even been born and others were still very young. So it may come as a surprise to many that social networking wasn't even a 'thing' then, and a phone was something in one's home or office with a wire that attached to a wall outlet. As all-things-related-to-computing exploded, so did social networking; smart phones appeared in every hand and landlines became almost-extinct dinosaurs. But apparently God didn't get the memo, because He's been networking from the beginning of time, and He doesn't need either a phone or other computerized gadget to make it happen. It's not unusual that one person will get a prophetic word, revelatory insight or have a dream, only to find out later that the Lord had already been speaking similar, or even identical, messages to others at or around the same time – social networking God's way. This is that.

In *Dreamspeak,* I related a story of how God started with one of my dreams and developed a whole computer scenario from start to finish, resulting in in the *Backdoor Prayer* in 2016, which is published in *Generational Prayers, 2022 Edition.* Why is that important to mention here? Because, testimonies from multiple people have confirmed that this prayer has made a difference in their lives. Also, as God's network expands, another as-revealed-in-dreams networking/computer scenario has recently become relevant.

Programs and utilities are always running in both the foreground and background on our phones, tablets and computers. Some of these are necessary for the system to function; but others may be malware, adware, or other malicious programs designed to hijack the device, often compromising personal information. We may end up with a device that is so overwhelmed with garbage that it becomes very difficult to sort out the underlying truth, because the surface reality we see is often false. Subscript programming is the true reality; it is that truth we need to discover as we delve into our dreams. God's truth is vital, as spoken by Jesus:

> *If you abide in my word, you are truly my disciples, and you will know the truth, and the truth will set you free.*[1]

The first indication we have recorded from Aslan's Place regarding such programming occurred in a dream that Paul had in 2015:

> I had a dream where I saw people but there was a subscript. I woke up and knew it was computer programing language. My interpretation is that the fallen sons of God are running a subscript behind what is happening.

Paul's son, Brian, is adept at computer science, so Paul asked for his thoughts:

The official definition for subscript is (of a letter, figure, or symbol) written or printed below the line. Subscript is also used in computers to run more than one process 'program' at the same time. So in your dream, this could represent how a person could be speaking and acting one way, but at the same time, doing something completely different.

As the years went by, more references to such programming often came up in ministry sessions. Then, toward the end of November 2022, I received the following email from Paul:

Two nights ago I had an obsessive-compulsive dream, like an endless loop featuring high-end fashion designers. The emphasis was on Christian Dior. I would wake up and think, "Why I am obsessing with this?" I finally had to get up and walk around, hoping this would get rid of the endless loop of the dream.

Yesterday, I had a session with a Korean couple. The Lord exposed a dragon over Korea; and it seemed that the dragon was over a larger area of Asia, but the heart of the dragon was in Korea. Somehow we started taking about subscript programming; I asked if the Koreans were obsessed with fashion, especially Christian Dior. I was stunned when she told me that fashion really was an obsession, but she didn't know about Christian Dior. I did a search and found this article from 2021,

Mysteries in the Night

Dior's Revenue in Korea Jumps More than Twofold Despite Pandemic:

> French luxury fashion house Christian Dior racked up 104.7 billion won ($93.2 million) in operating profit last year despite the coronavirus pandemic, according to data from the financial supervisory service.
>
> Christian Dior Couture Korea, the operator of the brand's South Korean unit which produces clothes, bags and makeup products, also saw its revenue rise 75.8 percent to 328.5 billion won, while its net profit jumped by 250 percent to 77.7 billion won...
>
> At department stores, casual outfits and suits for women suffered respective 32 percent and 26.1 drops in revenue, driving down overall sales.
>
> Revenue for luxury brands, however, rose by 15 percent from the previous year, becoming the only category in the department store sector to do so apart from household goods.
>
> As the pandemic prolonged, "revenge spending" emerged as a new shopping phenomenon in Korea in which shoppers would buy expensive items as an alternative to international holidays to compensate for the lack of reward "to compensate for the

> disappointment caused by unexpected stressors like the coronavirus lockdowns, shoppers, particularly mid- and high-income people, tend to spend lavishly on rare luxury goods"...[2]

It seemed that the dragon was imposing an identity on the Korean couple, an identity tied to fashion. It is a kind of programming. Like in my dream, the people are locked into this system and can't seem to get out. I wonder if this is tied to the religious spirit that seems so prevalent in the Korean church.

Apparently, God's version of social networking was very active, for on the very same day Rob Gross also had a dream, which he thought was very strange:

> I dreamed this morning of going into Macy's, or perhaps a fancier store like a Nordstrom's, and walking into a part of the store that displayed high-end fashion clothing. I was welcomed by a nicely dressed female sales clerk. Notable about me walking into this area, was that I purposely decided to visit this part of the store, never having gone there before. It was as if I decided to explore it for some reason.

Within days, at least three of us had experienced endless-loop sort of dreams. Mine happened two days after Paul's:

> I awoke early today from a dream in which there were three ongoing threats, which seemed to cycle

round and round, progressively getting worse. But suddenly, one was completely resolved and I knew that the other two were empty threats. My husband, who I suspect represented Jesus, was with me in the dream, and in the resolved threat he was both my protector and the one who had the solution.

I went back to sleep for a couple of hours and endured another endless cycle, this time seeing Amazon orders on my computer of things I hadn't ordered and didn't want - over and over and over. There were prompts coming up that I've never seen on Amazon, but didn't know if I should use them because I didn't know if they were valid prompts or if I'd been hacked.

Talking with Paul about both of our dreams, it seems we're onto something new, with false realities cycling in dreams on top of the true subscript realities; like simulations that hide God's truth. In his repetitious fashion dream, the true reality was realized the next day when he prayed with the Korean couple and researched the Korean fashion problem; that being that God was aware of the cultural problem and wanted to deliver them.

In my dream of continuous-cycling threats, it appears that the Lord broke through the false reality with true reality of His presence and protection. But what of the Amazon dream? I don't know yet, but is it possible that was meant to spark my imagination so I would add to this previously-finished chapter? Perhaps; but wait, there's more.

About the same time, our friend Byron, who is an Aslan's Place intern, asked if he could send me his eight-year-old daughter's dream. He'd already spoken with Paul, who had discerned and prayed about ungodly connections to things pertaining to some very complex spiritual insights; some of which had been revealed in recent ministry sessions that included Byron as member of the prayer team. The summary of Sadie's dream:

> Everyone was dropping their kids into a large pit with mud and slime at the bottom. There was a specific timing to drop them so that they could be saved by these cauliflower-like platforms. Sadie and her sister fell into the pit at the wrong time but were saved by Santa. But there were those who weren't told about the proper timing of the cauliflower platforms and put their kids in at the wrong time when they couldn't be saved.

The purpose here is not to explore all of the interpretive aspects of the dream, but to illustrate God's creativity. Note the convergence of networking that doesn't require computerized devices, with parental guidance for kids and their dreams, with subscript/true realities in dreams.

Byron reflects:

> Sadie was fixated on the kids being lowered into the pit. The striking thing to me was that we had lowered them as well. I got the sense of generational betrayal; there is a void between my generation and

my parents, and between them and their parents, all set up by the enemy.

Everyone in the dream was sending their kids down and no one was exempt - believers and non-believers alike. We were all participating, unknowingly, in a systemic problem; something seen as normal or accepted by society. Lord, How am I sending my kids into the pit??? I think it has to do with the generational void.

I asked for as much detail as I could from Sadie. There was a long pause, and then she suddenly remembered the second part of being saved by Santa arriving on his sleigh. This was met with lots of joy and thanksgiving on my part. We may not be able to save our kids from our generational programming, but Jesus will. The gift-giver (Santa) is key. I got, "Do not fear the oncoming destruction and the current gap between generations; put your trust in the ultimate Giver and His ultimate gift."

This dream came the night after we discerned intense evil in a prayer session.

Isn't that amazing! An eight-year-old had a dream that was somehow tied to the things her dad has been discerning, but from a kid's eye view. Then, Dad spent time with his daughter, helping her to explore what probably would have otherwise been a frightening dream to discover the underlying truth, or subset reality, that Jesus, disguised as Santa, was there to help her.

I am in awe of the complex manner in which God put all of this together:

- At least three of us experiencing endless, looping dreams within days of one another
- Paul exploring the issue of co-existing false realities and true/subscript realities seven years before the current dreams
- Paul, along with a ministry prayer team including Byron, delving into complex new revelatory insights from the Lord
- A Korean couple being set free in the midst of unfolding revelation
- Byron's timing in sending his daughter's dream to me; completely unaware of my dreams, or that it might fit into this discussion
- The wonderful example of a father training up his child in regard to dreams; and comfort for both of them as he encouraged her to delve deeper into this specific dream, where she discovered the true reality of Santa (Jesus) to the rescue, the subscript reality of His truth that He is the Savior

Our God is truly an awesome God who weaves incredible tapestries throughout both the waking and sleeping hours of our lives:

O kingdoms of the earth, sing to God; sing praises to the Lord, Selah to him who rides in the heavens, the ancient heavens; behold, he sends out his voice, his mighty voice. Ascribe power to God, whose majesty is over Israel, and whose power is in the skies. Awesome is God from his sanctuary; the God of Israel – he is the one who gives power and strength to his people. Blessed be God! [3]

And he who searches hearts knows what is the mind of the Spirit, because the Spirit intercedes for the saints according to the will of God. And we know that for those who love God all things work together for good, for those who are called according to his purpose. [4]

There can be no doubt:

If you abide in my word, you are truly my disciples, and you will know the truth, and the truth will set you free. [5]

---

[1] John 8:31-32

[2] https://www.koreaherald.com/view.php?ud=20210407000784

[3] Psalm 68:32-25

[4] Romans 8:27-28

[5] John 8:31-32

Chapter Thirteen:
Love Letters From God

Most of us have probably received a love letter at one time or another. Perhaps it was a romantic one from a love interest; or perhaps it was a valentine or other greeting card from a good friend or family member. The ultimate love letter, available to all, is God's Word, the Bible; but He seems to love to sneak in some reminders of His love for us while we sleep too. King Solomon wrote:

> *It is in vain that you rise up early and go late to rest, eating the bread of anxious toil; for he gives to his beloved sleep.*[1]

One night, I'd been consciously focusing on a pursuit of God in His righteous depths when I first went to bed. I'd fallen asleep briefly and had a very short dream or vision – not sure which. I sensed I had entered into a cave that was very deeply hidden in God's depths; and inside there were emeralds.

With no knowledge what the emeralds meant, I opened a dream book the next morning to look it up. The first thing I saw on a random page were the words, 'cut and uncut stone', but there was no such listing under 'c'; so I looked at 'stone'. Sure enough, it was there; an uncut stone means ordained by the Spirit and an emerald, among other things, often refers to mercy or praise. I loved that, and recorded my side of a conversation with the Lord in my journal:

> As I'm trying hard to pursue You, Lord, You give me a flash of something I never could have thought of to confirm that Your Spirit-ordained praise dwells in secret places in Your righteous depths. I didn't even know that I was praising You in my attempts to explore them, yet that's exactly where I ended up! Thank You!!!

I believe that every dream that is of God is one of His love letters. Yes, some of them may seem difficult because they reveal generational sin issues or, as previously seen, prophetic warnings; but those are truths, spoken in love by the Lord because He wants to help us overcome harmful issues in our lives.

> *When the Spirit of truth comes, he will guide you into all the truth, for he will not speak on his own authority, but whatever he hears he will speak, and he will declare to you the things that are to come. He will glorify me, for he will take what is mine and declare it to you. All that the Father has is mine; therefore I said that he will take what is mine and declare it to you.*[2]

Others among the Lord's love-letter dreams may be prophetic, in keeping with His words:

> *For the Lord GOD does nothing without revealing his secret to his servants the prophets.*[3]

Then there are dreams that inspire us to pray for situations and/or other people. How He must love us not only to cherish our prayers, but also to answer them!

A Fresh Perspective on Dreams

> *When I shut up the heavens so that there is no rain, or command the locust to devour the land, or send pestilence among my people, if my people who are called by my name humble themselves, and pray and seek my face and turn from their wicked ways, then I will hear from heaven and will forgive their sin and heal their land.*[4]

> *But I say to you, Love your enemies and pray for those who persecute you.*[5]

> *Therefore I tell you, whatever you ask in prayer, believe that you have received it, and it will be yours.*[6]

Think about it; there are as many reasons for a dream as there are reasons why God might want to talk to us. With that in mind, an examination of your dreams may reveal buried treasure, perhaps even emeralds hidden in the depths of His endless love,.

> *Give thanks to the LORD, for he is good, for his steadfast love endures forever.*[7]

---

[1] Psalm 127:2
[2] John 16:13-15
[3] Amos 3:7
[4] 2 Chronicles 7:13-14
[5] Matthew 5:44
[6] Mark 11:24
[7] Psalm 136:1

Mysteries in the Night

Chapter Fourteen:
And Yet, there's More

As has happened before in previous books, I thought I was finished; and yet, God had more to add. A few days ago, I had a sense that I was supposed to ask Briana to pray about whether or not the Lord wanted to give her a prophetic word regarding this book, and yes, He did. But apparently He wanted to deliver more than just a word, and added a dream into the mix.

From Briana:

After Barb asked me if I had a prophetic word for her book, I asked the Lord and felt that I would get something at 6AM the next morning. Around 4AM, I awoke and just waited while talking to the Lord. Then, I fall back asleep and had this dream around 6AM:

> I'm in a dark field at night wearing a bedraggled wedding dress.
>
> The scene changes, and I am now in a big public place; like an airport, where I have just gone through security and don't have socks or shoes or underwear on. I am pulled out of line by a security guard and taken with a small group of others to another part of the massive airport to wait. It seems we are being investigated or checked out for some

reason, and we are removed to another location until we are cleared.

My friend Tobias is with me and he shrugs it off laughingly; but I am furious because I am uncomfortable and lacking basic necessities, and the security guard is mean and has made a mistake.

When we get to the other side I begin to look for underwear and socks and shoes to buy, all of which I am lacking.

A woman comes up to me who is clearly possessed and asks me if I know about speaking to spirits; her daughter is with her. I stand up and lock eyes with the woman and say, "Yes, I know all about speaking with demons and spirits; and understand how they sometimes won't leave even when it seems you've tried everything. Trying to get them to leave sometimes even makes things way worse, and it's because the Key, the missing Key, is Jesus; and He is the only one who can set you free. Then He comes and fills you where the demons and spirits were before, and He makes you whole.

I had locked eyes with her as she backed away, and now I reached out and touched her head. She fell back with force as the evil left her and the power of God came on her.

A small crowd had gathered, and everyone was astonished because they knew who she was and how she would wander around asking others to communicate with spirits.

She came up changed, healed and delivered; and I began to disciple and teach her some basics of faith in Jesus. As I gave her my card so she could contact me if she needed anything, I noticed that the crowd that had gathered was now massive. It seemed as if they were mostly religious people, and oddly enough I recognized some from my own past.

There was a very tall young man in his 40s who was named Scott. He had medium-blonde, curly hair and glasses; and he began to talk to me about his troubles having to do with demonic oppression, but was nervous to speak to me for fear of being judged or misunderstood. He knew Jesus, and I shared that there is no shame in moving into new levels of freedom and how sometimes throughout our lives we have to deal with yucky critters that have entered us either because of generational sin or our own sin. I explained how it's a process of peeling back , and there's no shame or condemnation in getting free.

I touched him and the power of God came on him too; he also fell back with force, and was healed and delivered and we both knew it.

The crowd surrounded us now, and we became separated although I had more to say to him. The crowd was mostly curious, like it was this novelty for them, but there seemed to be no heart connection. But for the two, their lives were changed forever.

The security guard came back and I thanked God for derailing my day for this moment. I ran after the young man to give him my card, knowing that he would need to be discipled, especially in this religious atmosphere. People from my old church and my family members pointed him out as he was leaving.

Together, Tobias and I went back to where we'd been derailed by security. I was surprised to look down and see that I was finally appropriately dressed with socks and shoes and underwear, although I do not know how this happened!

As Barb and I prayed through the dream, we had these thoughts:

- Perhaps the beginning of the dream with the ragged wedding dress in the field was a picture of me in the religious environment that I came from, but which I am no longer a part of

- I remembered that Tobias' name means, "God is good". So, God's goodness went with me; and it also reminds me of how the Lord sent His disciples out two by two

A Fresh Perspective on Dreams

- God's goodness also laughs at the problems we face, as Tobias laughed at my irritation with the security guard in the dream

- Underwear socks and shoes appearing on me without either buying them or putting them on, indicates that God will supply my basic necessities and I won't even need to seek them out; so even though He may call me somewhere I feel totally unprepared to go, He will take care of everything I need as I obey

- Perhaps, I also did not need shoes where I was called to go, because my feet were covered with the preparation of the gospel of Peace; *as shoes for your feet, having put on the readiness given by the gospel of peace* [1]

- The missing, and later supplied underwear seems tied to scripture: *Therefore gird up the loins of your mind, be sober, and rest your hope fully upon the grace that is to be brought to you at the revelation of Jesus Christ* [2]

- The woman was there with her daughter, and the name Scott means someone from Scotland; so perhaps this indicates freedom for generations, and nations

- The curious crowd represent the current, 'give us a sign' people, just like the ones Jesus encountered;

> they have no true desire for freedom, but just want to be entertained

As I prayed through the above dream, I received the following prophetic word, which seems to reveal that not only was my dream perhaps an actual encounter, but also an invitation for all of us to experience divine interruptions and appointments in the night:

> This is about the harvest; this is about the bride; this is about the fields that are already white for harvest.
>
> Look inside and you will see the same power in Me that set others free.
>
> Lock eyes with Me, lock hearts with Me to set the captives free.
>
> Your dreams will increase and in the increase you will see what I am doing to set the captives free; for your dreams will become experiences, and your dreams will become encounters, and I will take you to places in the night that you have not known or bought a ticket for.
>
> Allow me to arrest your plans with mine, and soon you will see the heavenly traveling through the night, as the bride to the harvesting.
>
> Healings and deliverances and discipleship will begin to take place as you allow yourselves to have these heavenly encounters with Me.

A Fresh Perspective on Dreams

Spirit Airlines is unreliable, but as you learn to travel with Me in My Spirit, you will be surprised at the heavenly denial of injustice perversion and sickness in the land

And you will soon see, that traveling with Me on My Spirit Airlines, is the only way to rule and reign truly through the night.

For it is about MY Might and it is about My power, and it is about My end time harvest, and the revival of hearts that are turning to Me before the great and terrible day of the Lord.

So listen, all you who love His appearing; be patient and work and keep your lamps burning. Be faithful and ready and willing with Me to arrest the enemy and take them unawares; to astonish the religious and answer *their* prayers, and break the cells of unbelief where *they've* been held captive unwillingly.

For the obedience of one, and humility, will place you in places you did not want to go; but will nevertheless strategically take down the enemy and overthrow every plot assignment and plan to keep those from entering into their New Man.

This is about the harvest, so come work with Me; it's an invitation for all into what I'm building. Watch me and listen, look and wait for further directions into the night.

[1] *The Holy Bible: English Standard Version* (Wheaton, IL: Crossway Bibles, 2016), Eph 6:15.

[2] *The New King James Version* (Nashville: Thomas Nelson, 1982), 1 Pe 1:13.

CONCLUSION

As mentioned in the Introduction, there was only enough content to write a couple of chapters with which to begin this book, trusting and waiting on the Lord for everything else. As is evident, since there are a lot more than twenty pages, He came through again! No surprise, because He is always faithful; when He calls us to do something, He always equips us, just like He did with Moses:

> *But Moses said to the LORD, "Oh, my Lord, I am not eloquent, either in the past or since you have spoken to your servant, but I am slow of speech and of tongue." Then the LORD said to him, "Who has made man's mouth? Who makes him mute, or deaf, or seeing, or blind? Is it not I, the LORD? Now therefore go, and I will be with your mouth and teach you what you shall speak."*[1]

There can be no doubt that God's Word is a manual for every aspect of life, which should include our sleeping as well as waking hours. This is why, rather than concentrate on well-known dream scriptures, an effort has been made to integrate many passages from throughout the Bible that are not generally included in dream discussions.

My prayer is that you will have been blessed while reading this book, and that the Holy Spirit will have birthed new insights regarding God's gift of dreams and their interpretation. My earnest desire is that many will go on to

Mysteries in the Night

not only to understand their own dreams, but to teach others as well.

There can be no question that we are rapidly approaching the return of the Lord; time is short; so we would be wise to remember that dreams are important today:

> *And it shall come to pass afterward, that I will pour out my Spirit on all flesh; your sons and your daughters shall prophesy, your old men shall dream dreams, and your young men shall see visions. Even on the male and female servants in those days I will pour out my Spirit.*[2]

Mysteries of the Night: A Fresh Perspective on Dreams finally concludes with another prophetic word, this from my dear friend, Persis Tiner, a humble, elderly lady who is a giant in the Kingdom of God:

> Come dream
>
> Come dream with Me
>
> Let Me open secrets of the night, which will set you free
>
> Come open new realms yet unexplored
>
> My knowledge is limitless; My ways are many
>
> Come explore a fresh way with new eyes from above
>
> Come, let Me show you My many-faceted expressions of love.

A Fresh Perspective on Dreams

---

[1] Exodus 4:10-12

[2] Joel 2:28

Made in United States
North Haven, CT
31 January 2023